I am grateful to God for my life and for all the opportunities He gives me to start over. The year 2024 will certainly not end like the year 2023 did. As long as there is life, there will always be a new beginning.

Thank you for everything, Jesus Christ is the savior of my soul.
Thank you for everything, Jesus Christ is the love of my life.

Karina Franco - 2024

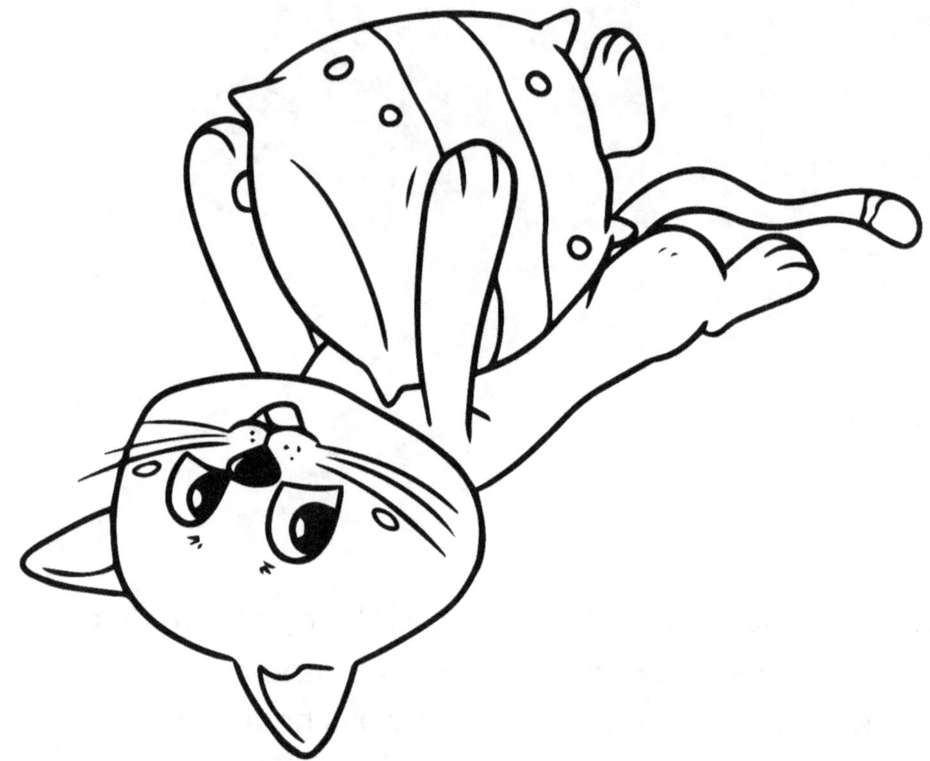

This Book Belongs to:

____

Test Color Page

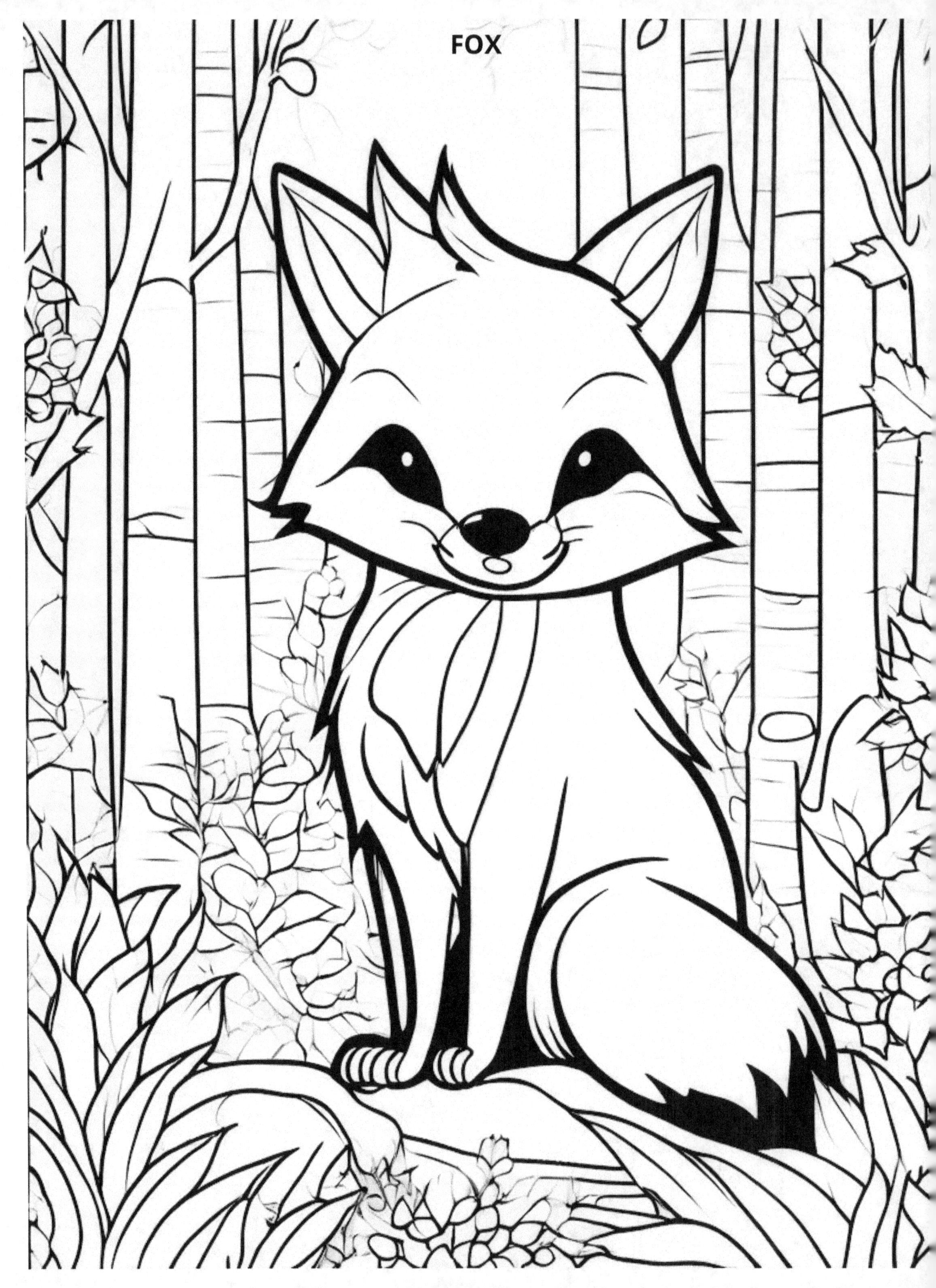
FOX

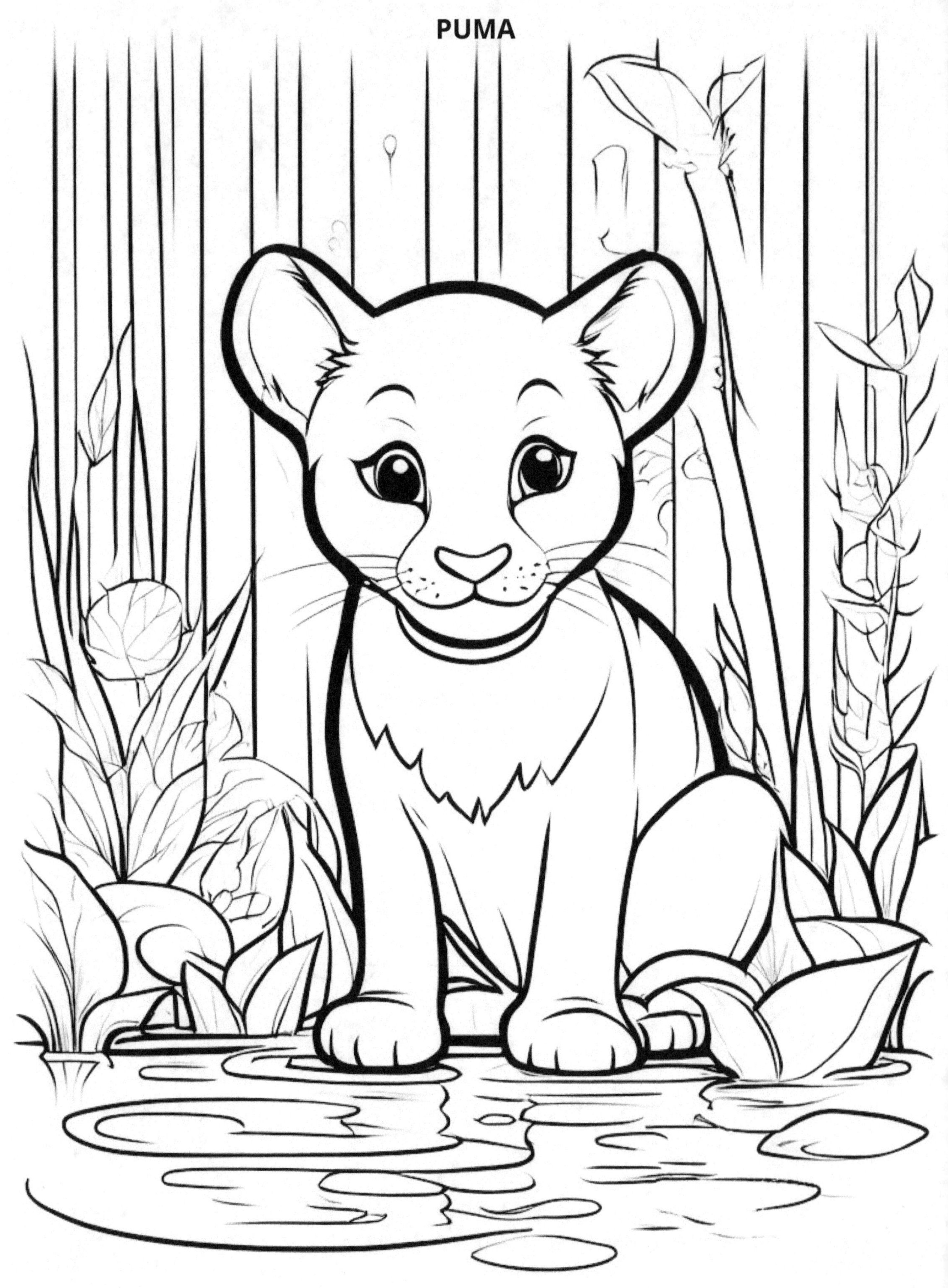

ALLIGATOR

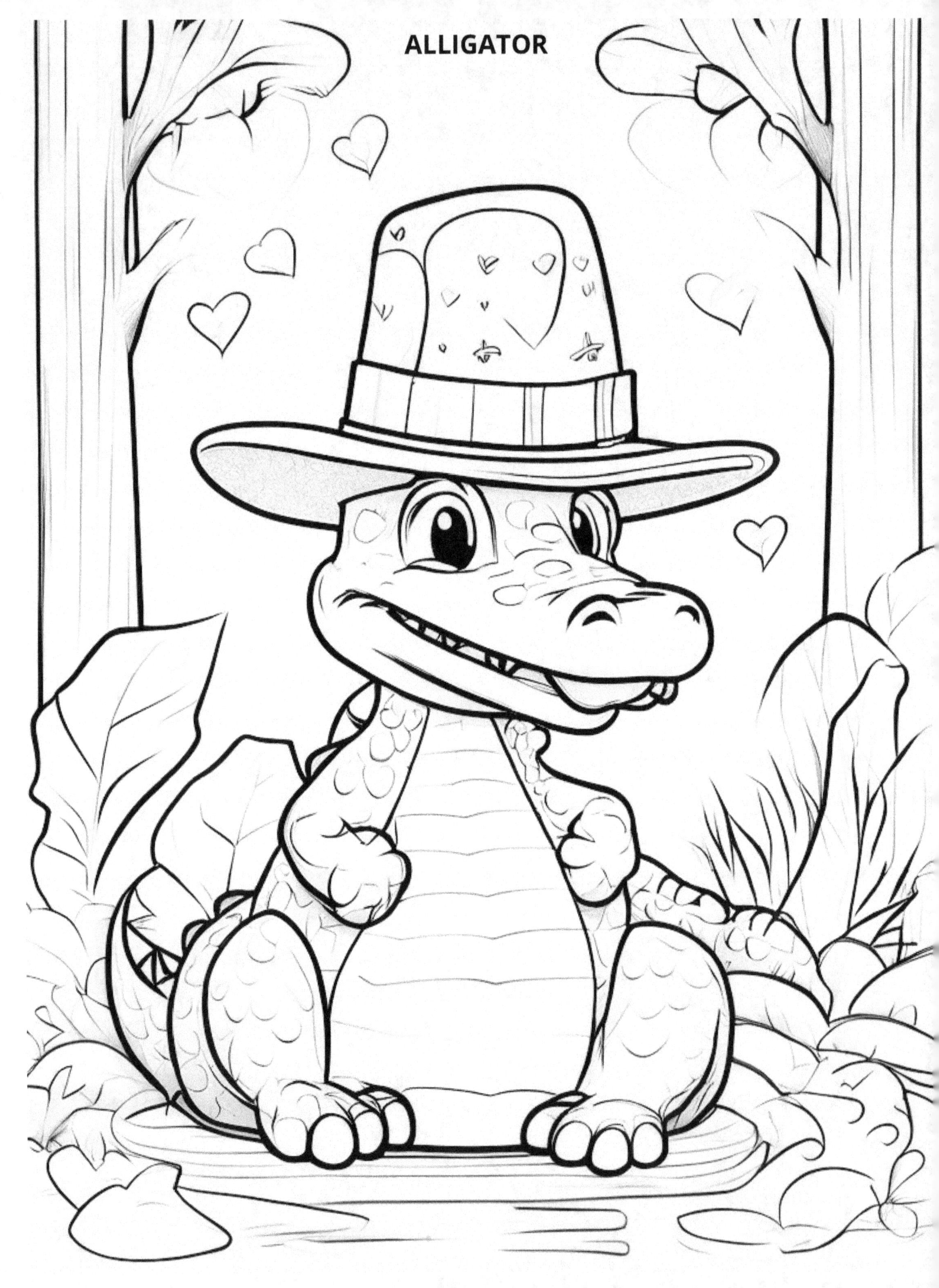

FROG

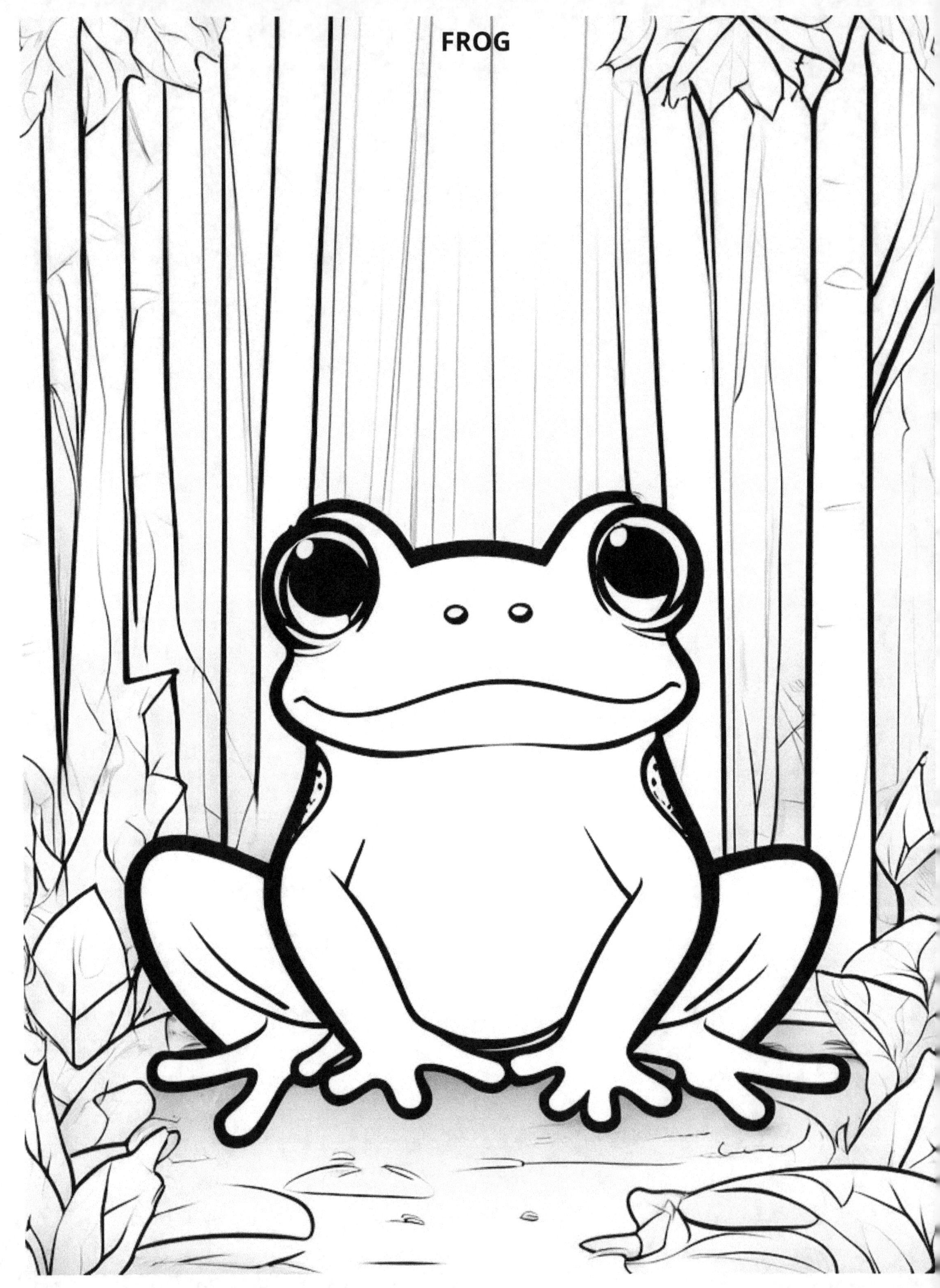

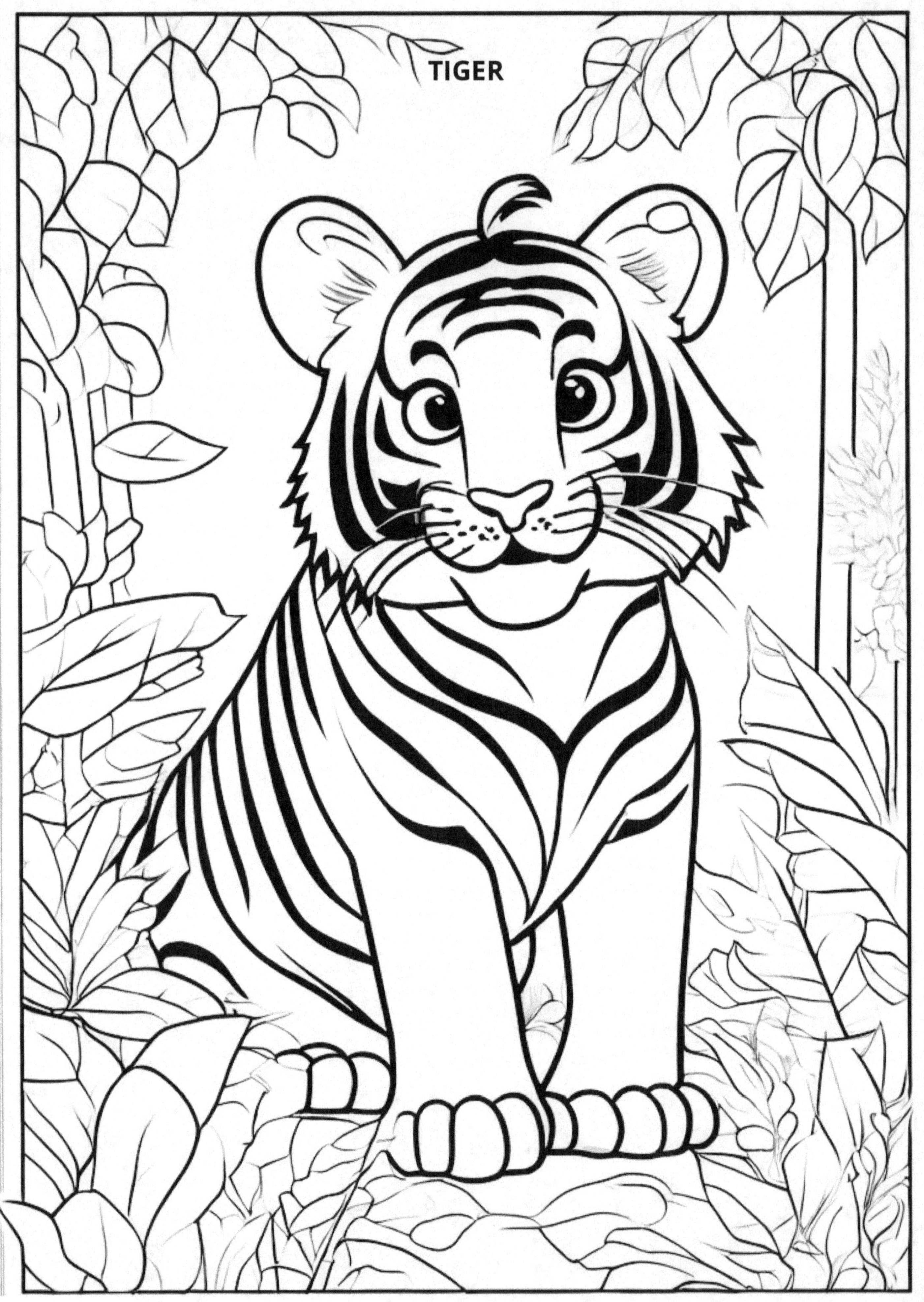
TIGER

BROWN BEAR

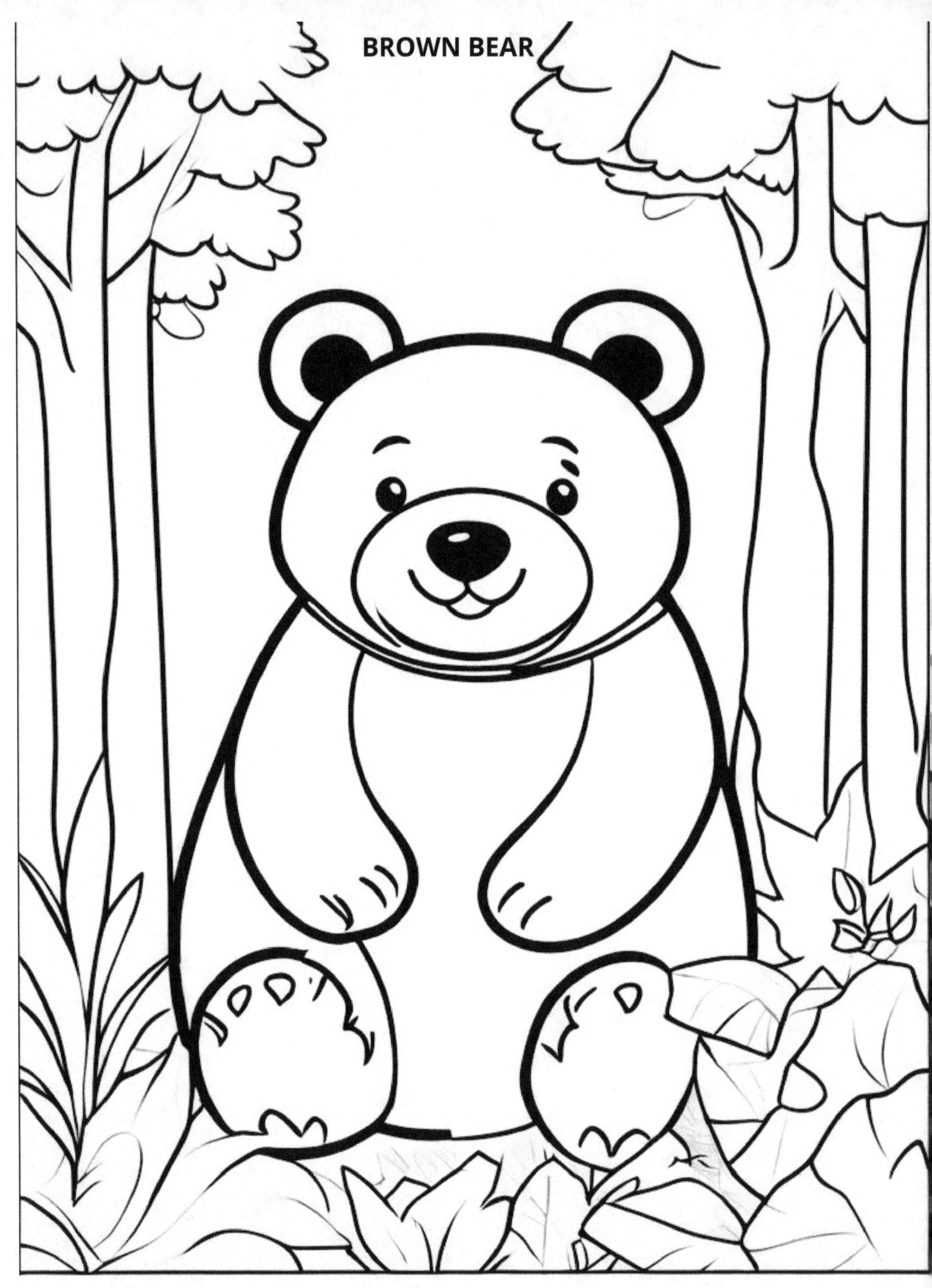

WOLF

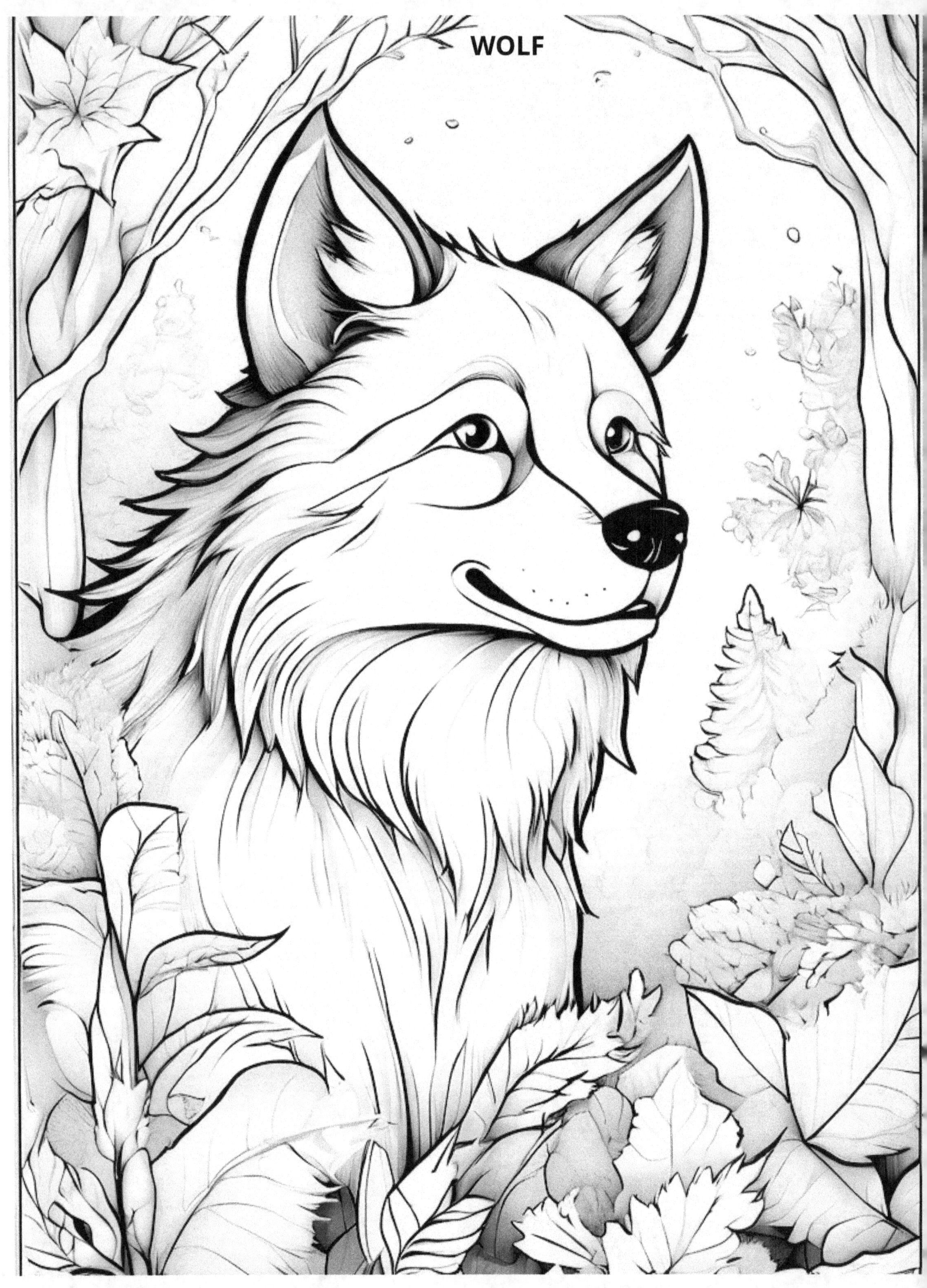

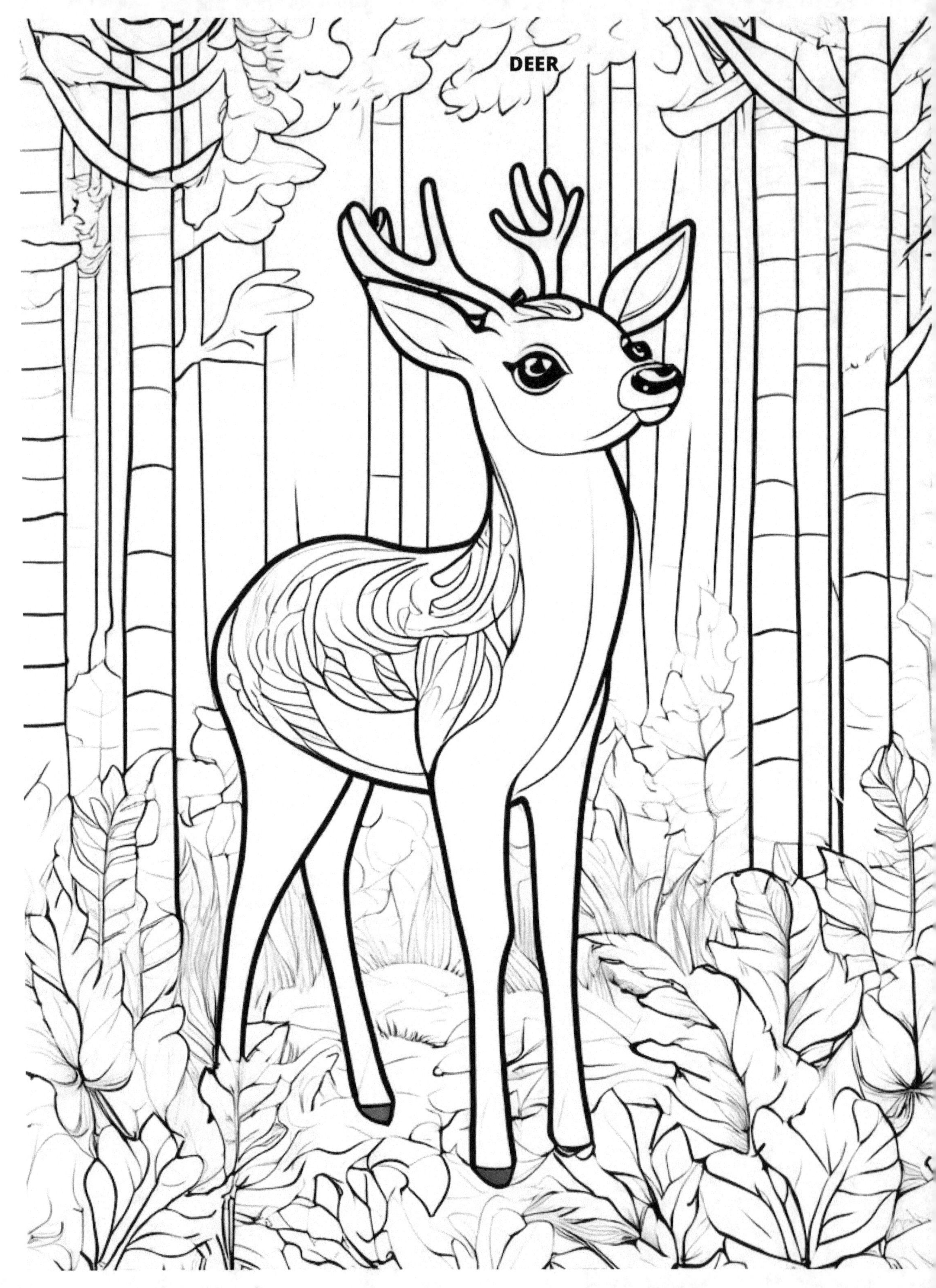
DEER

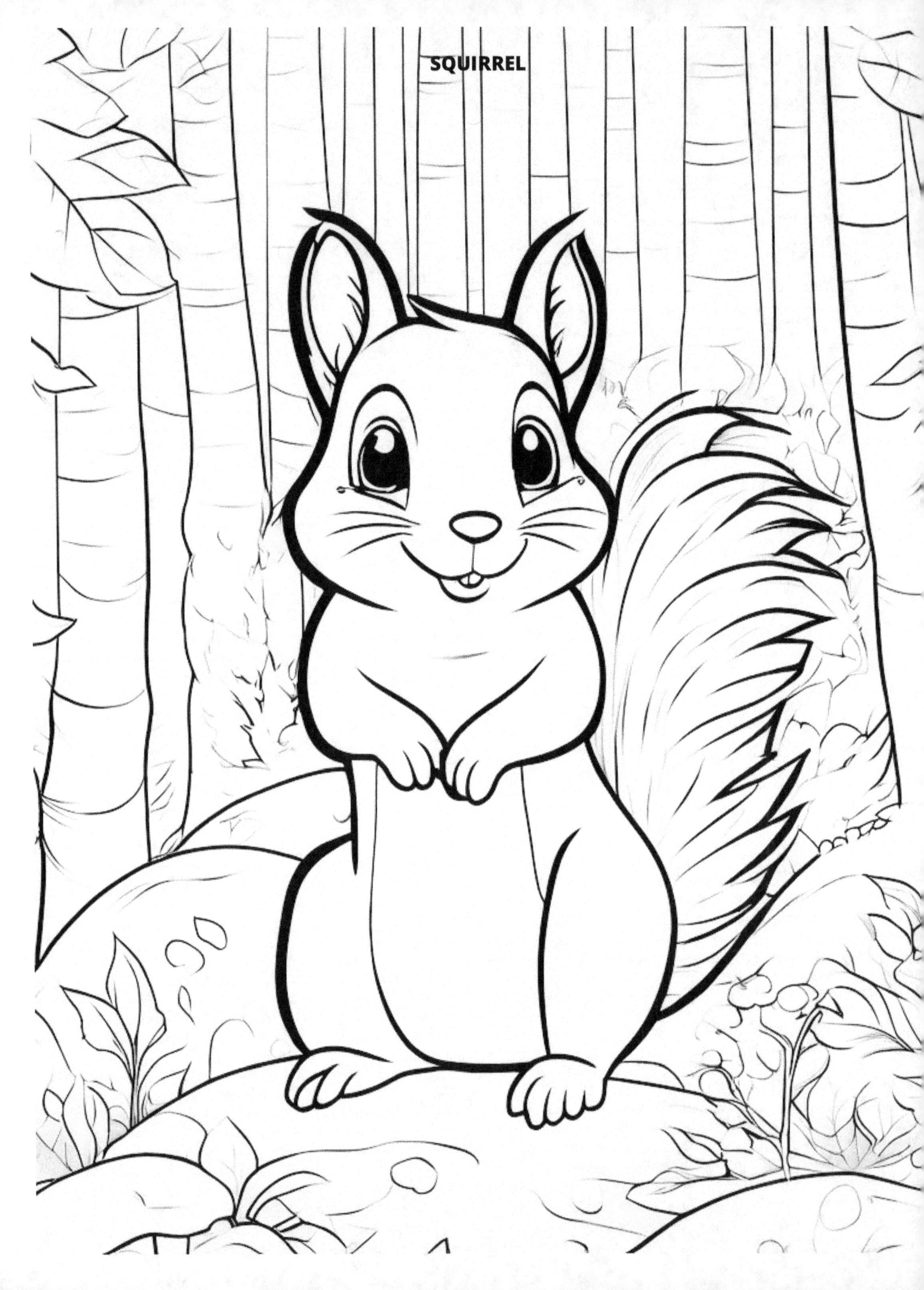
SQUIRREL

LEOPARD

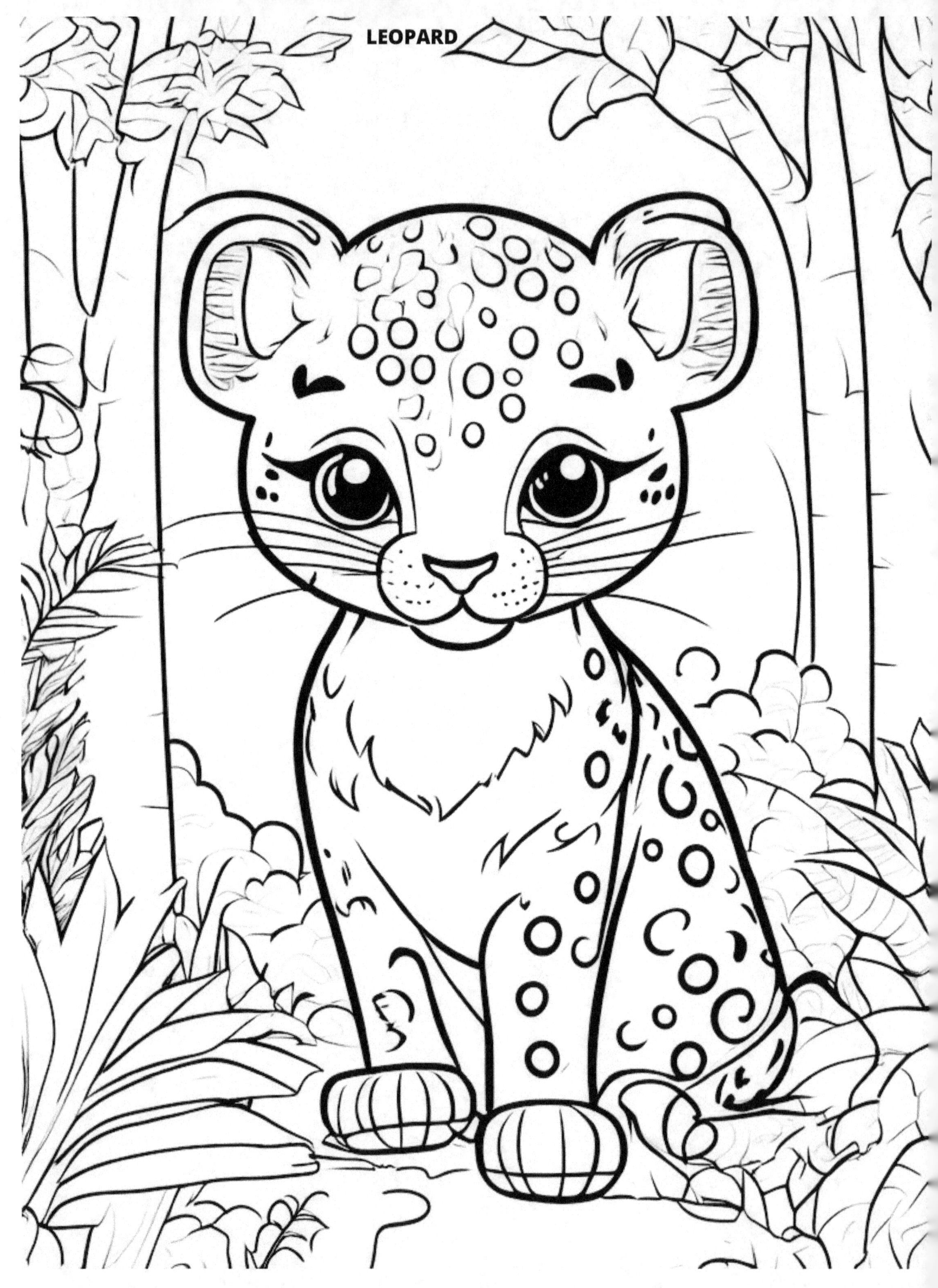

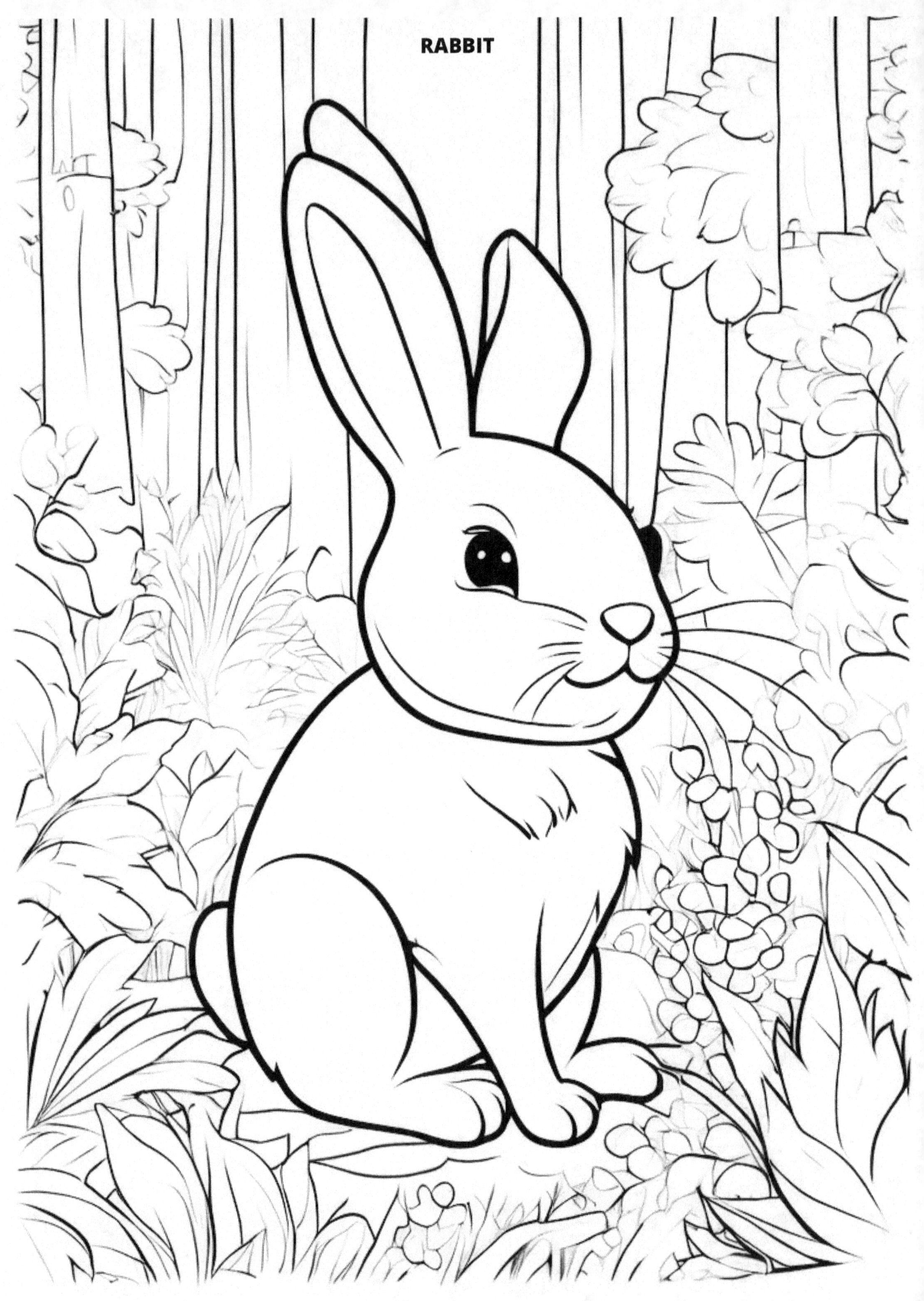
RABBIT

GORILLA

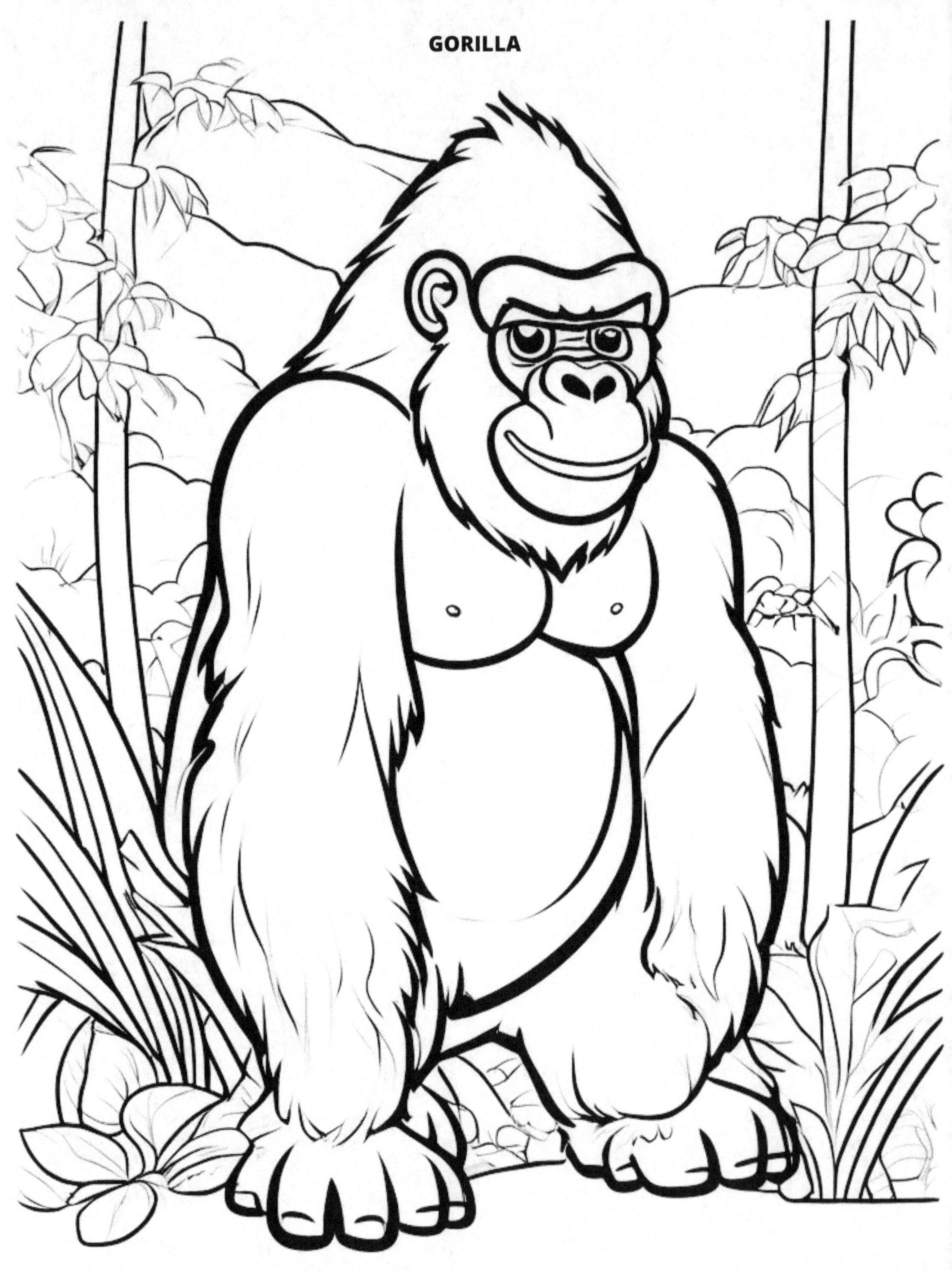

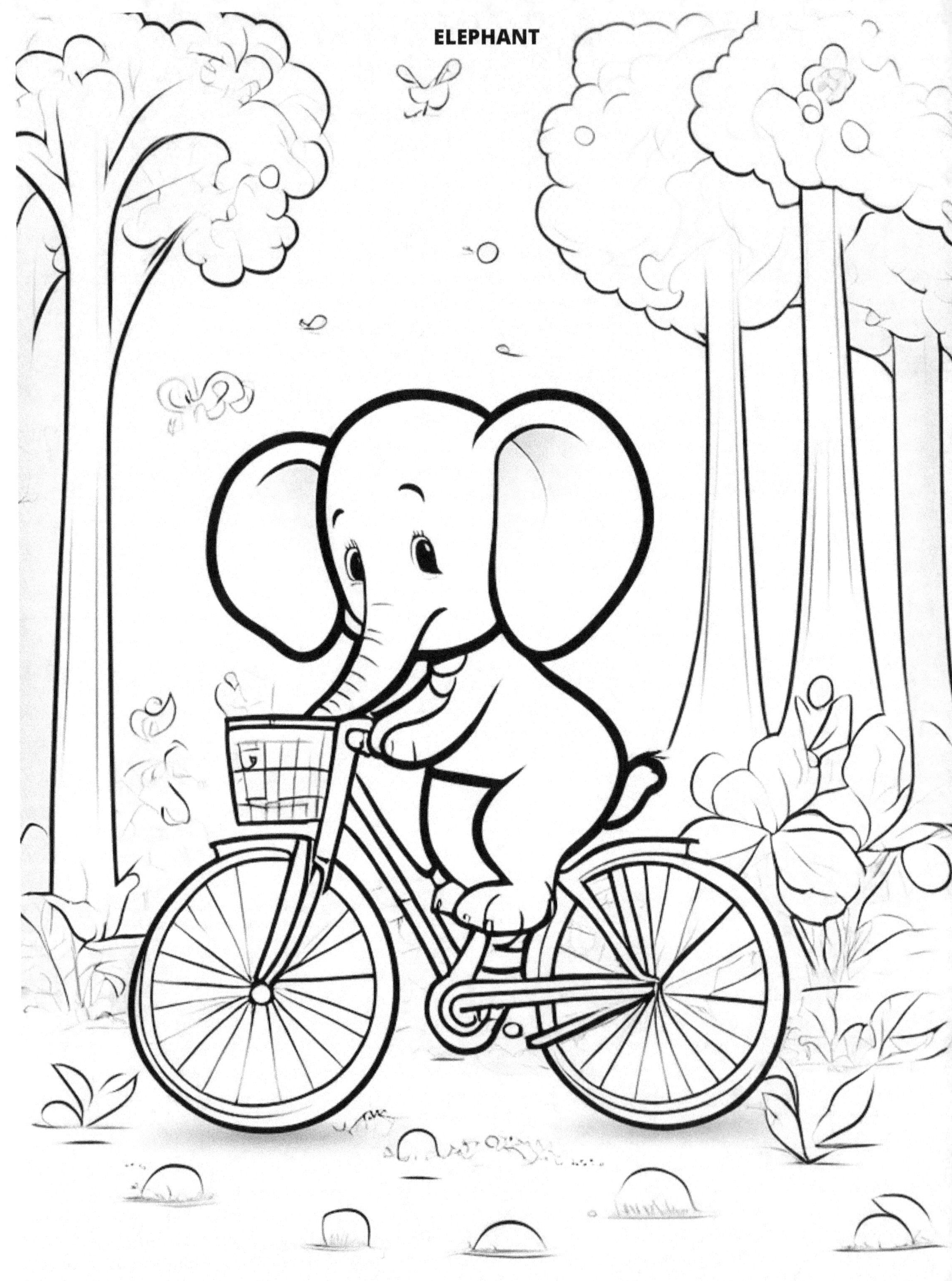
ELEPHANT

PANDA

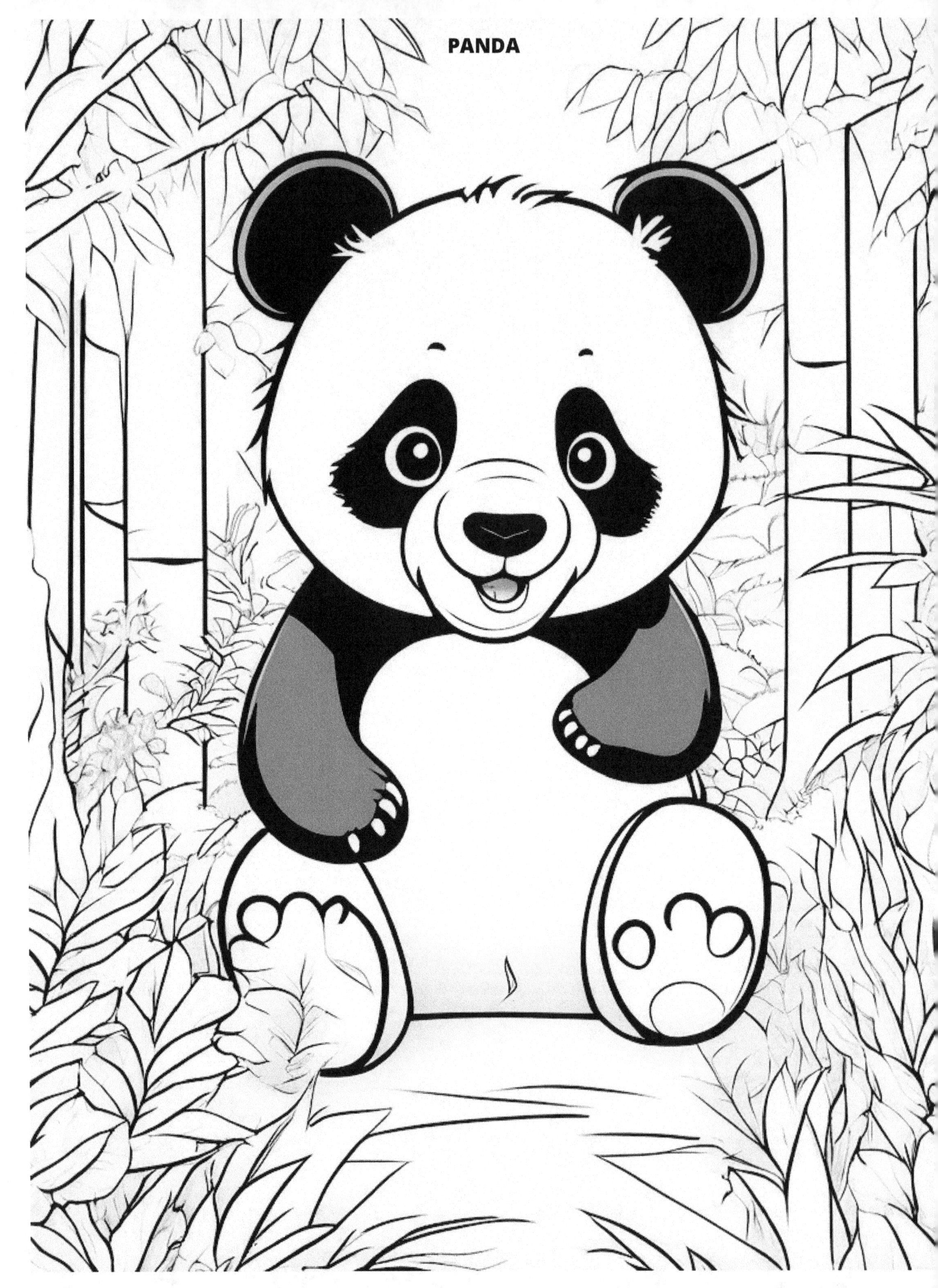

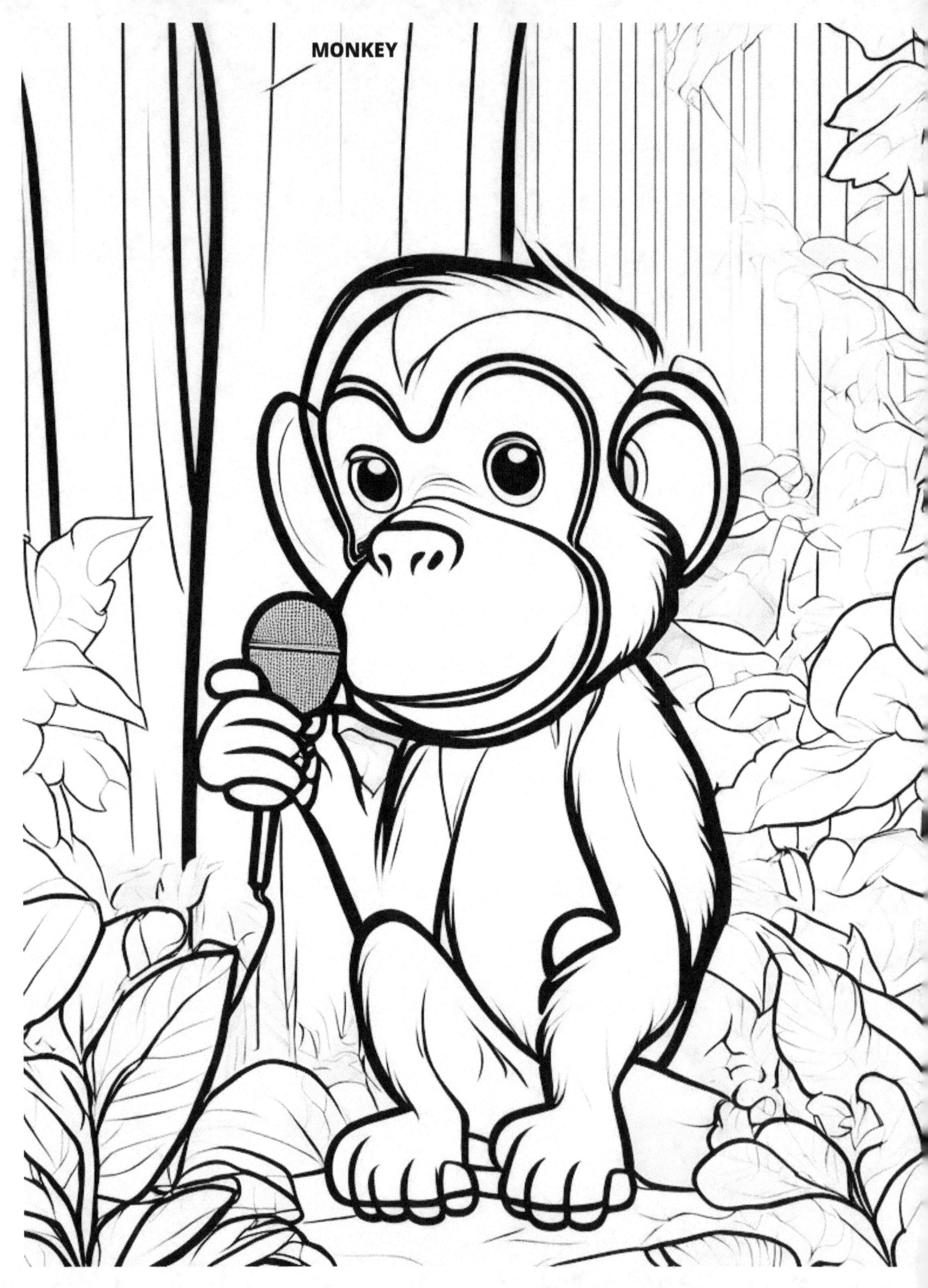
MONKEY

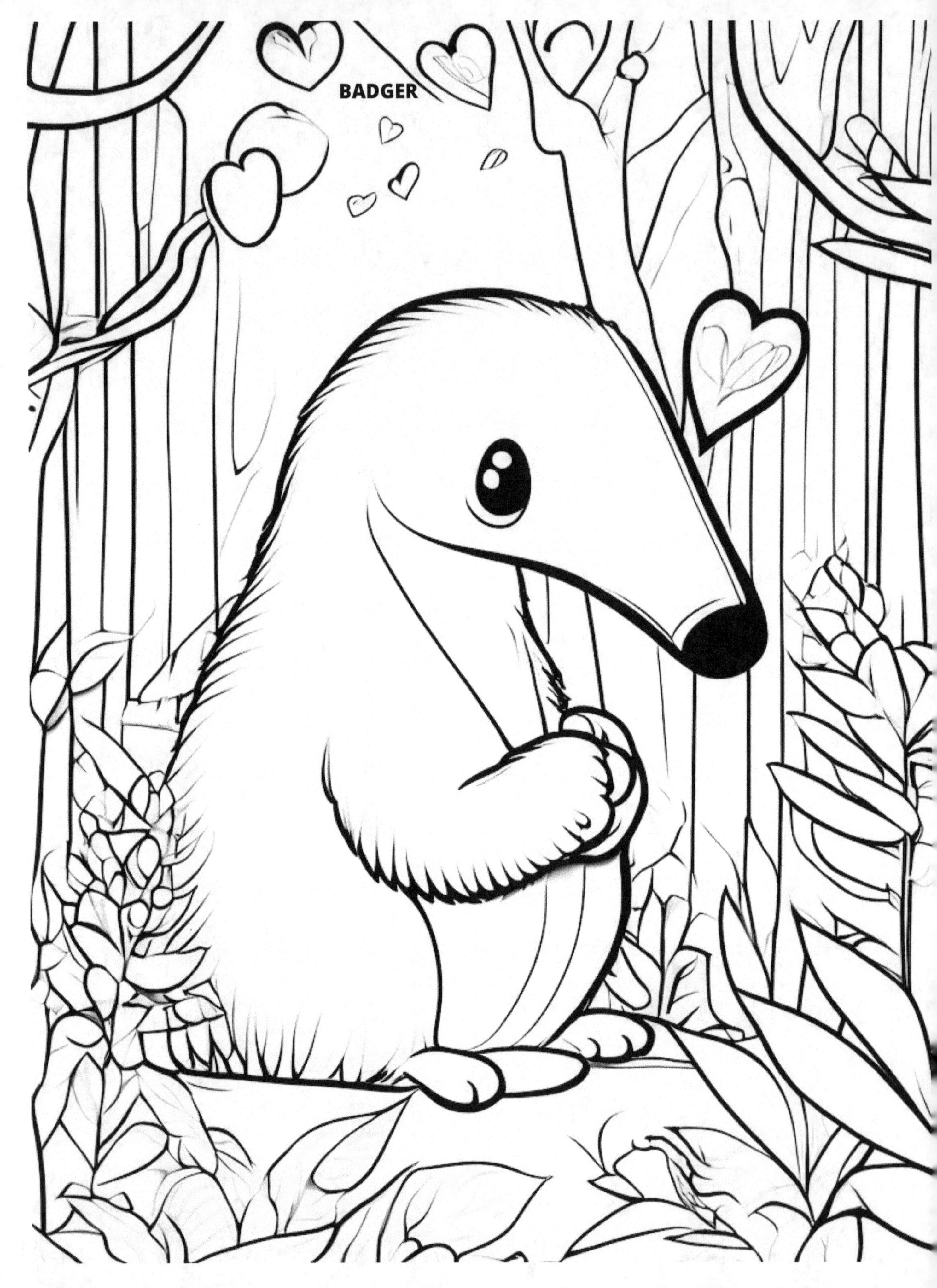
BADGER

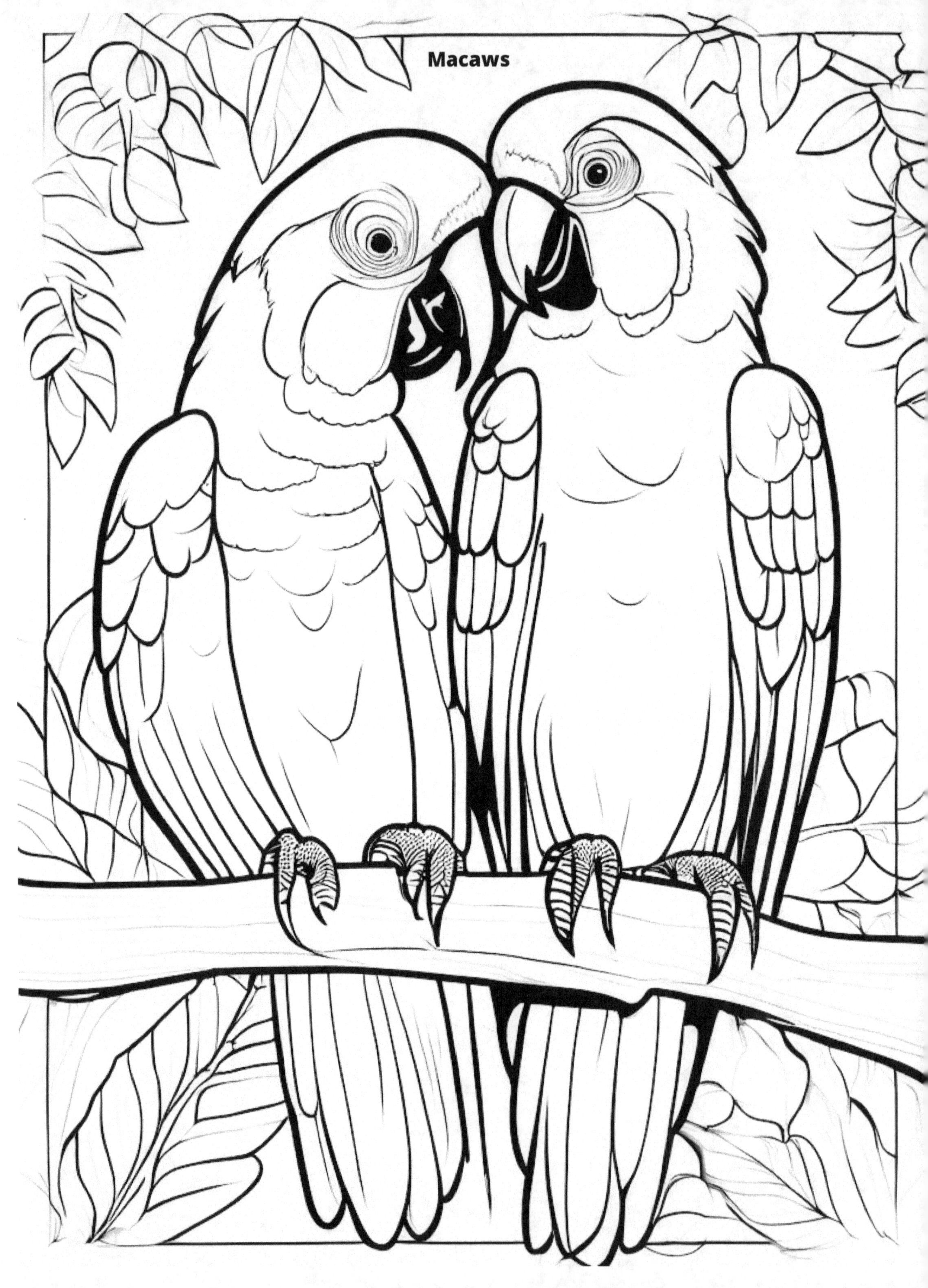

Macaws

JAGUAR

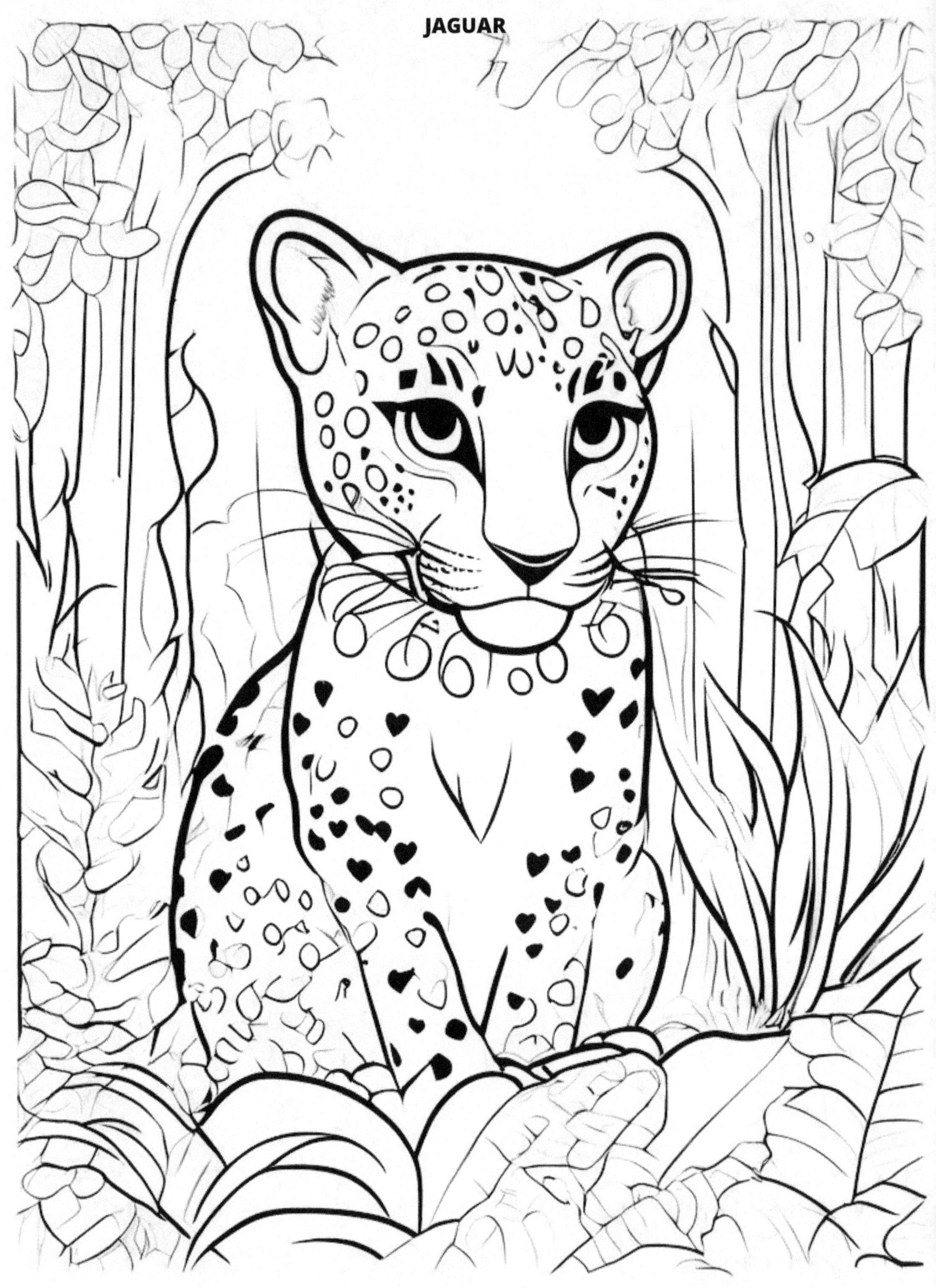

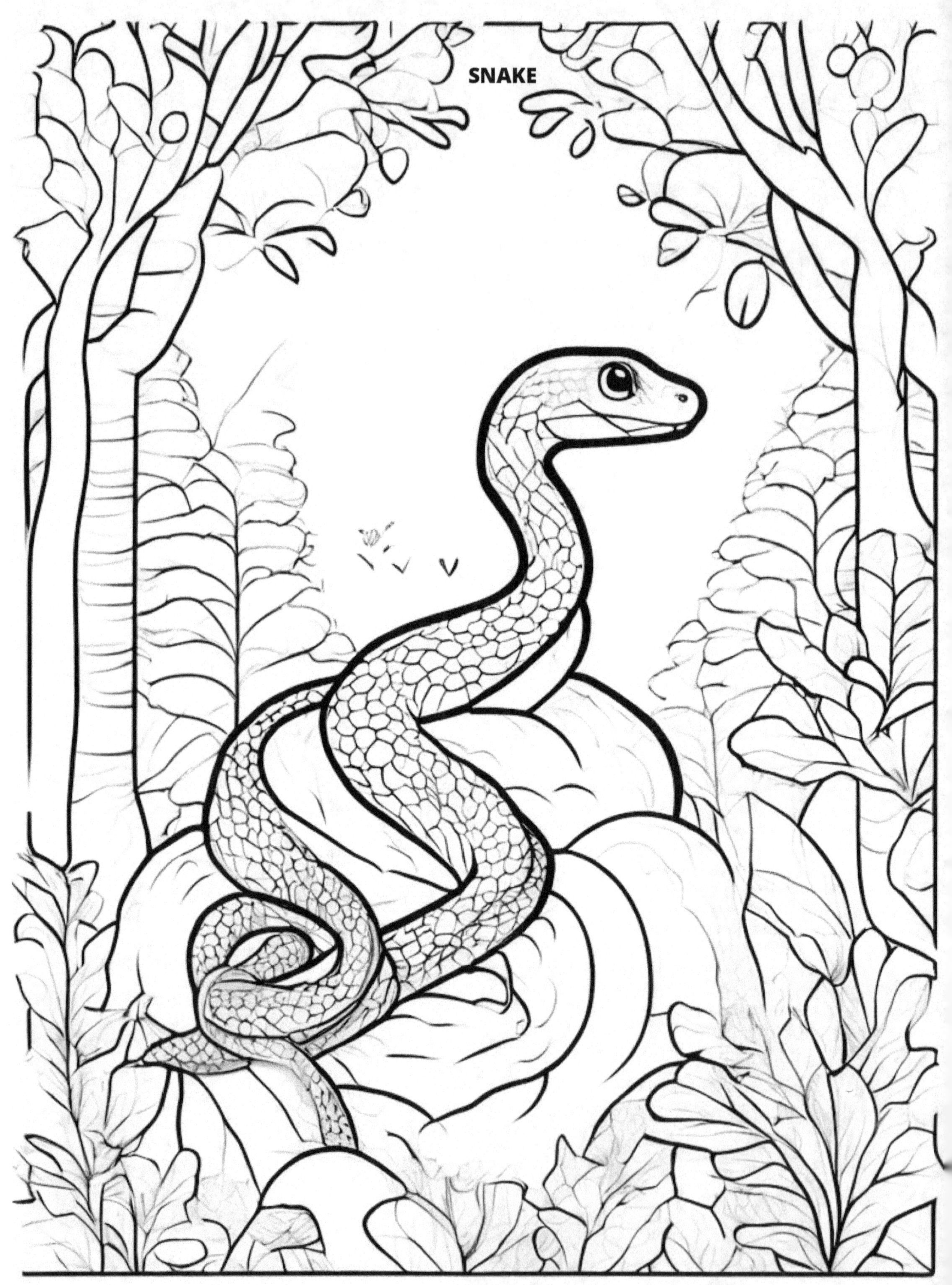
SNAKE

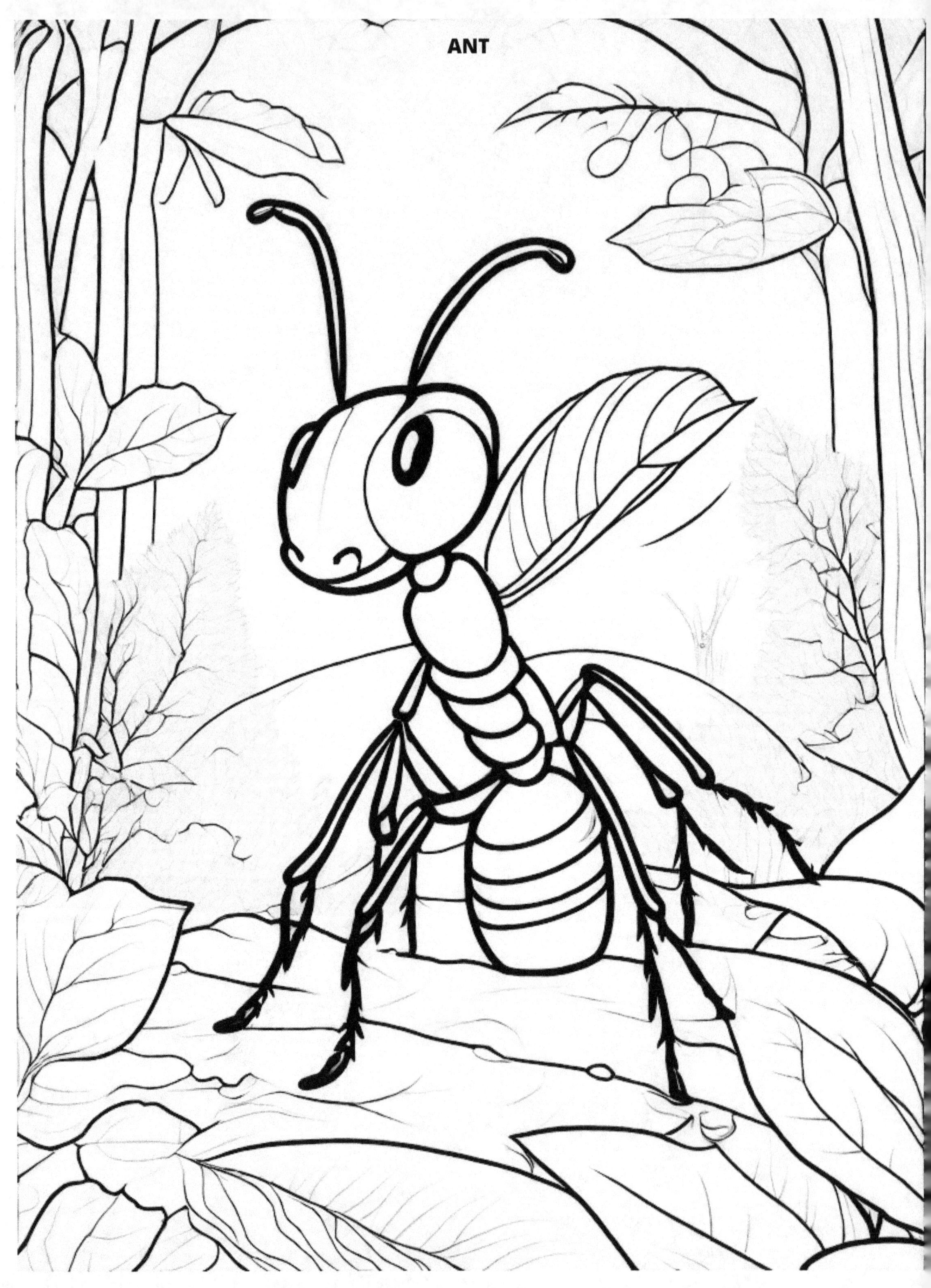

ANT

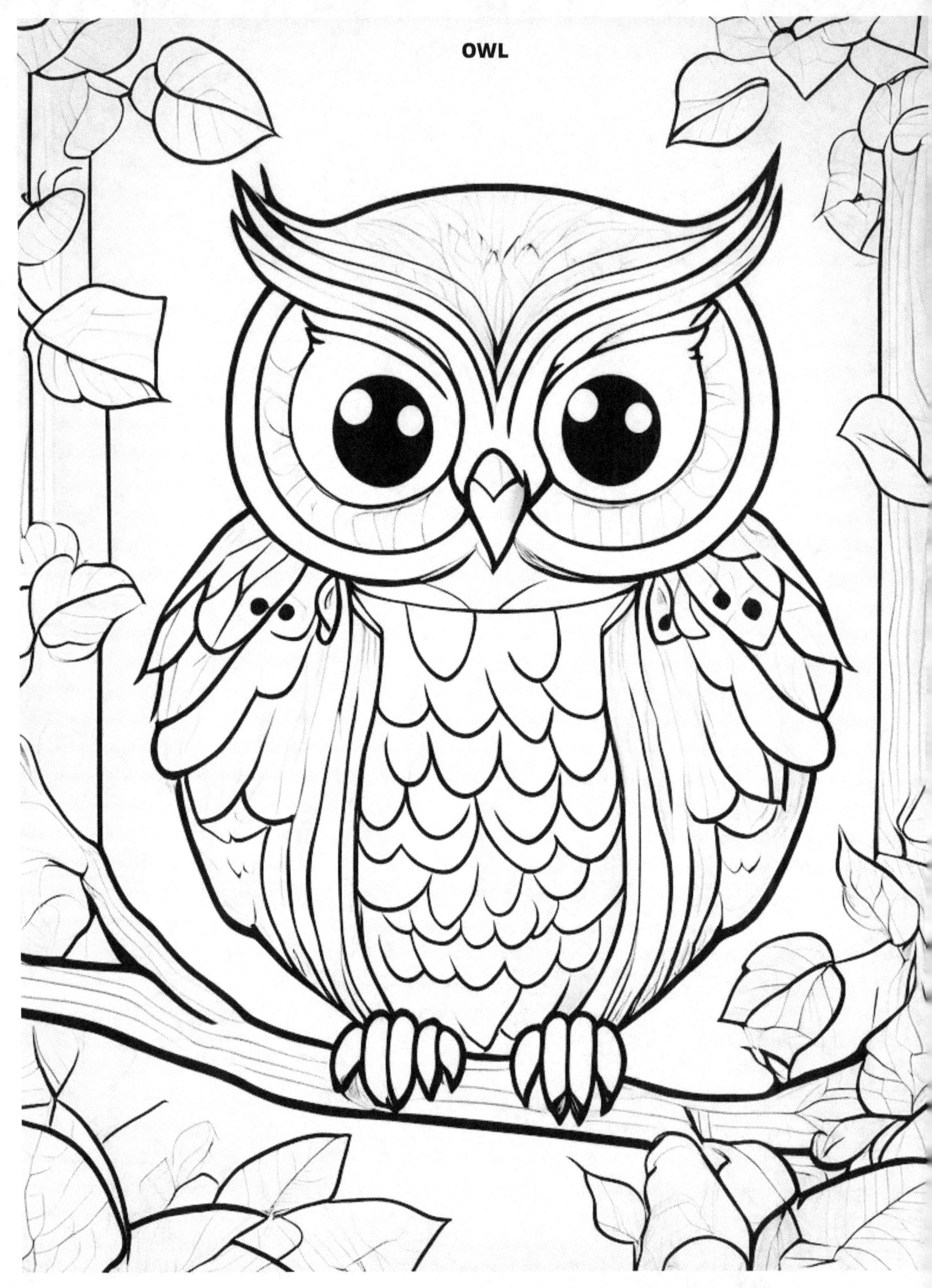

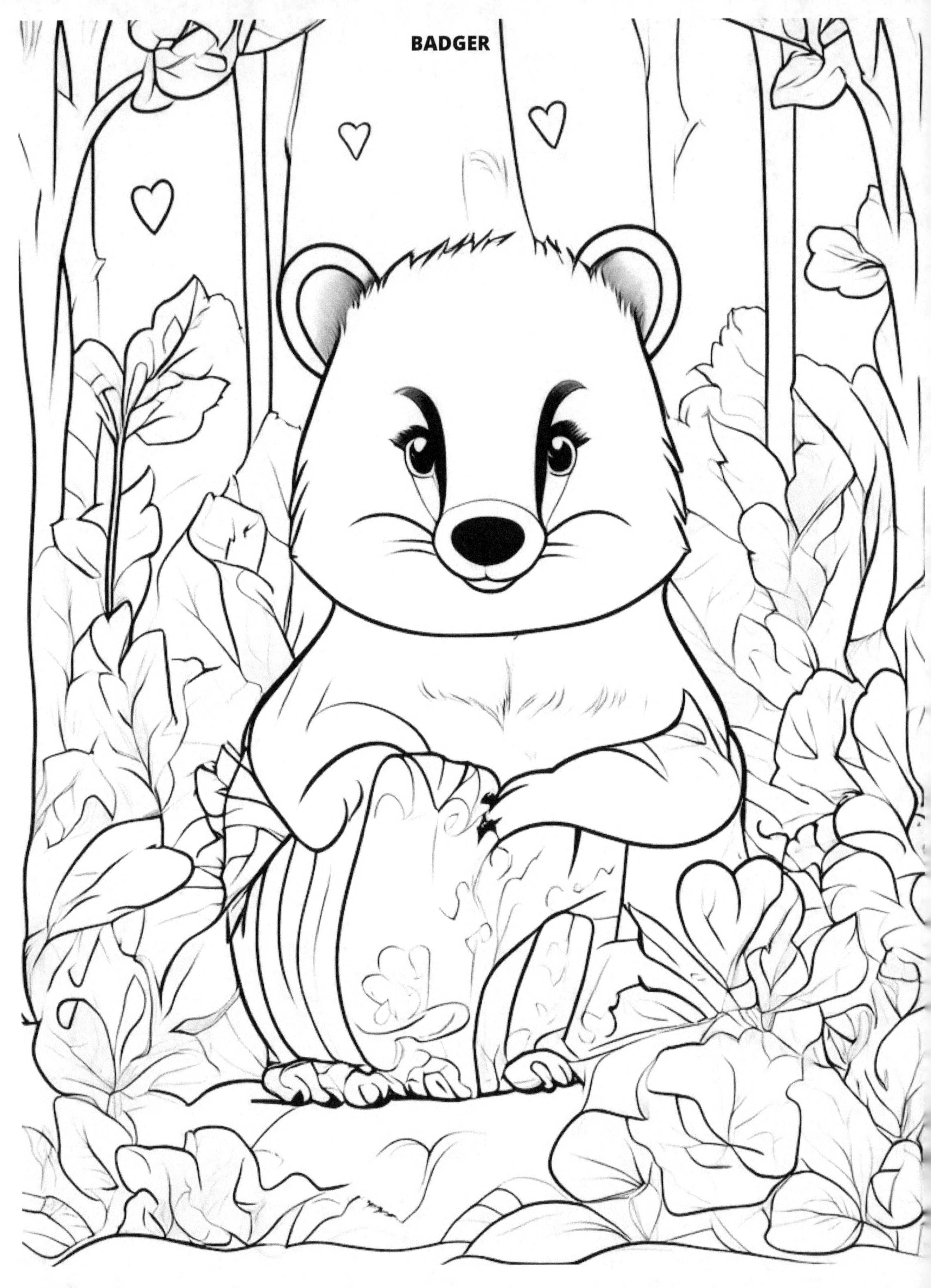
BADGER

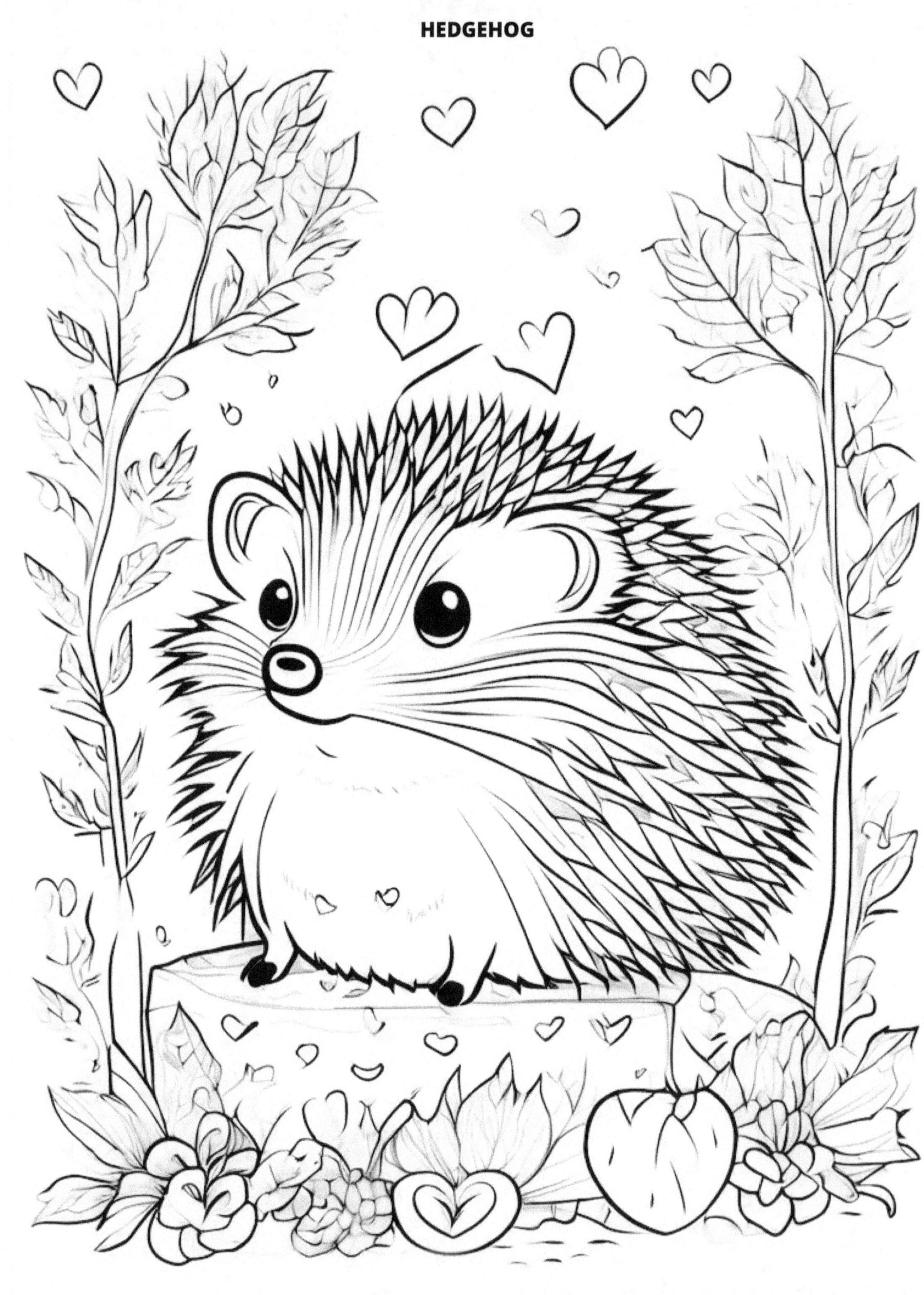

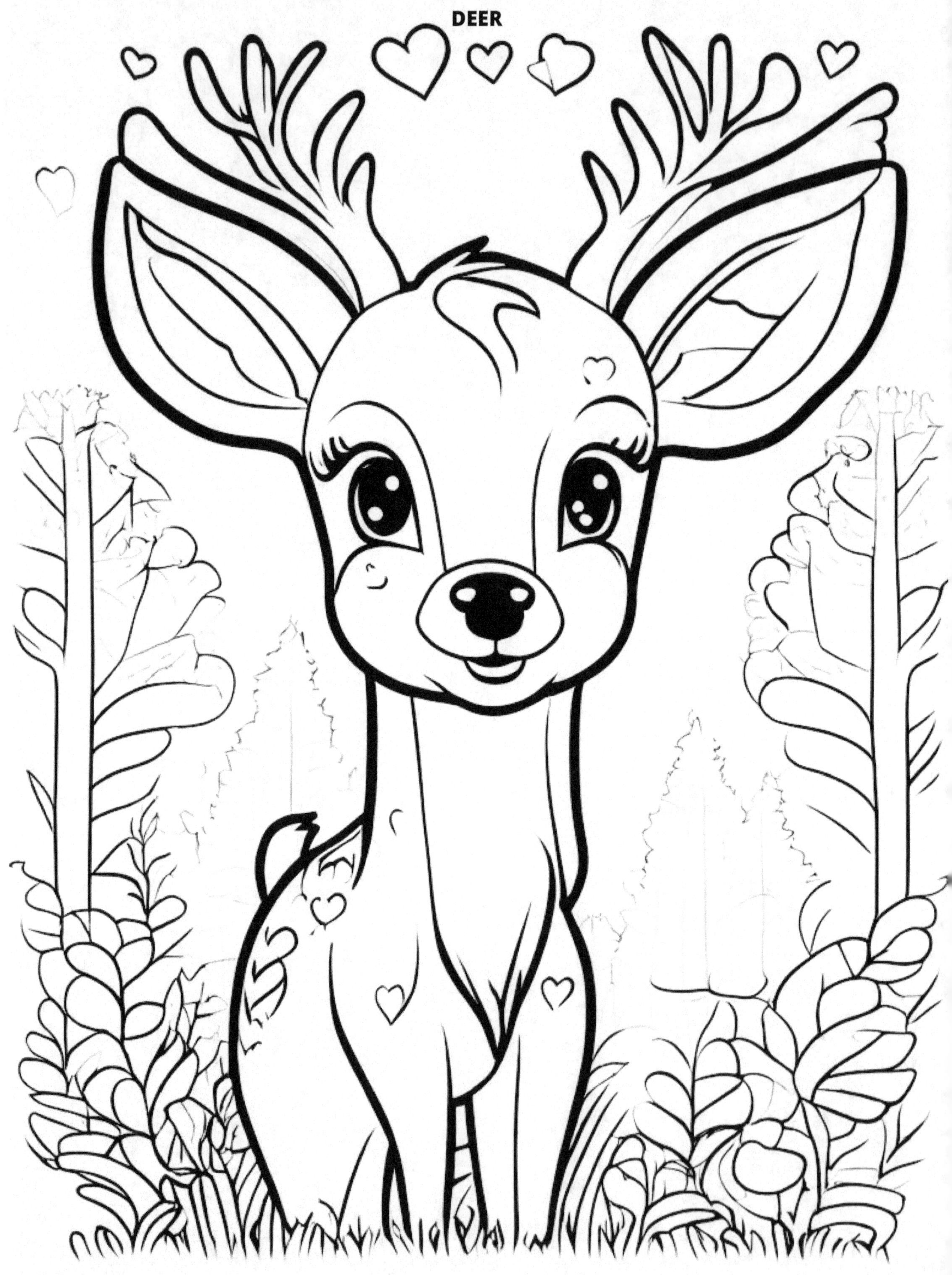
DEER

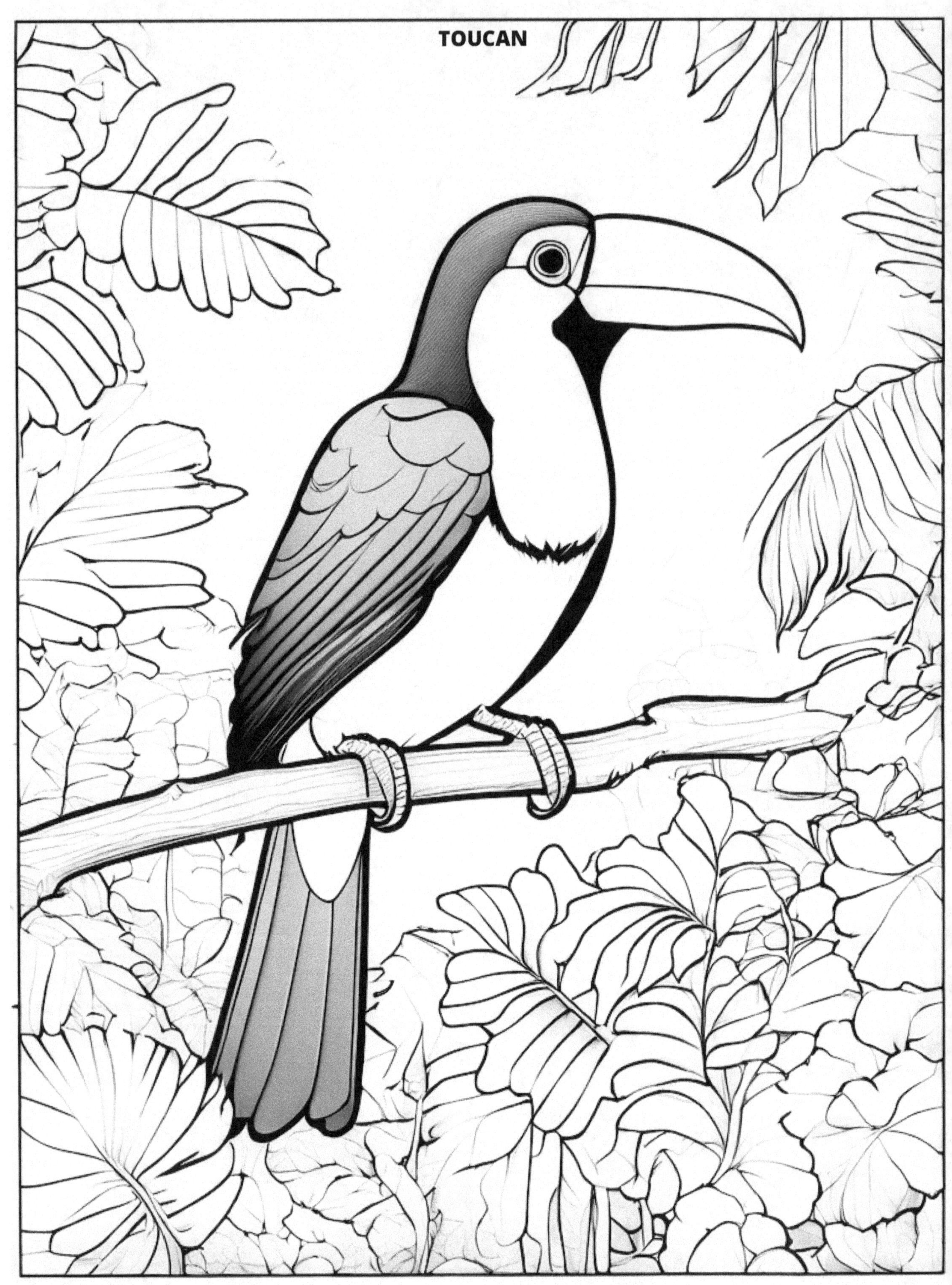

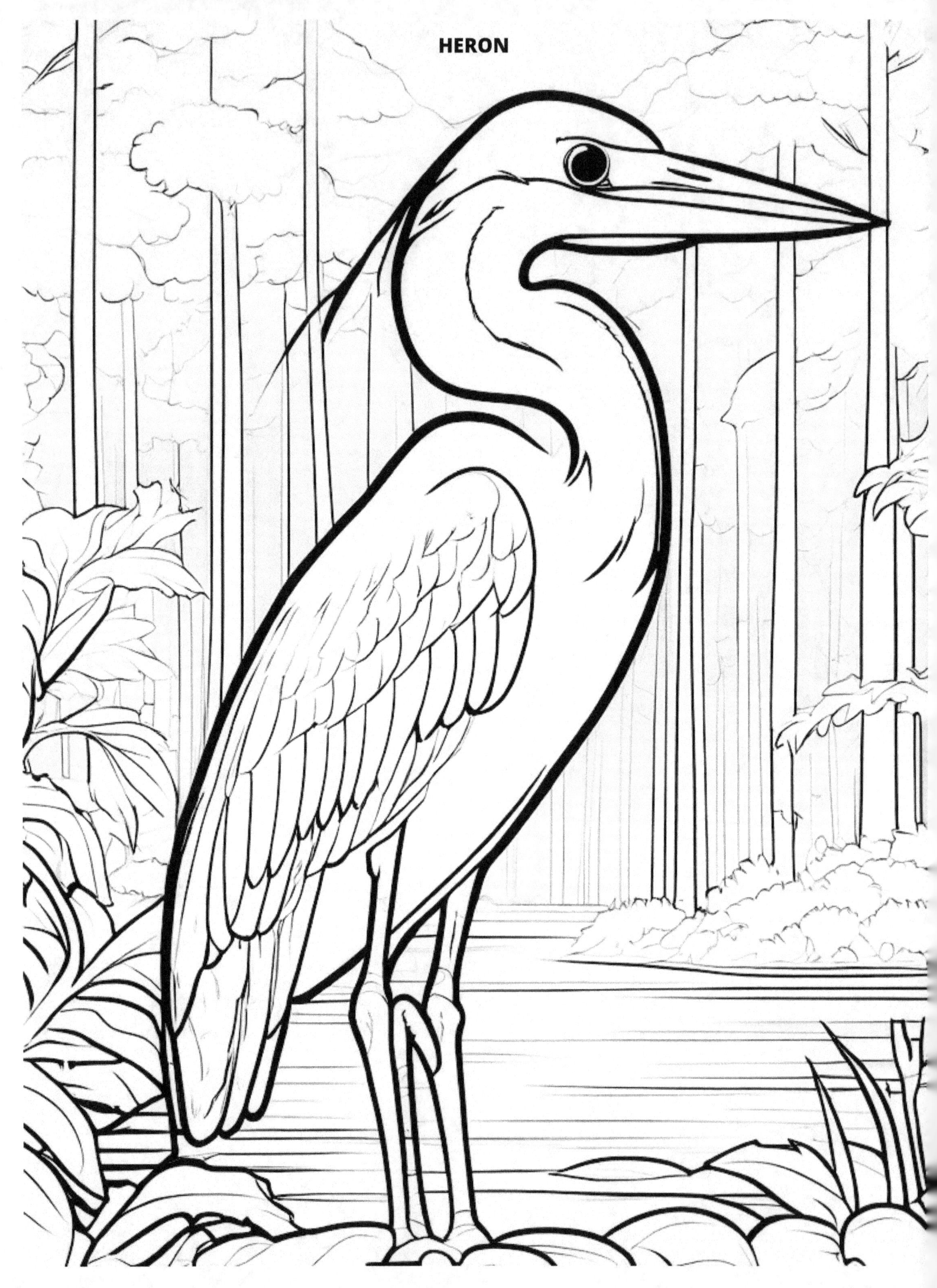
HERON

WEASEL

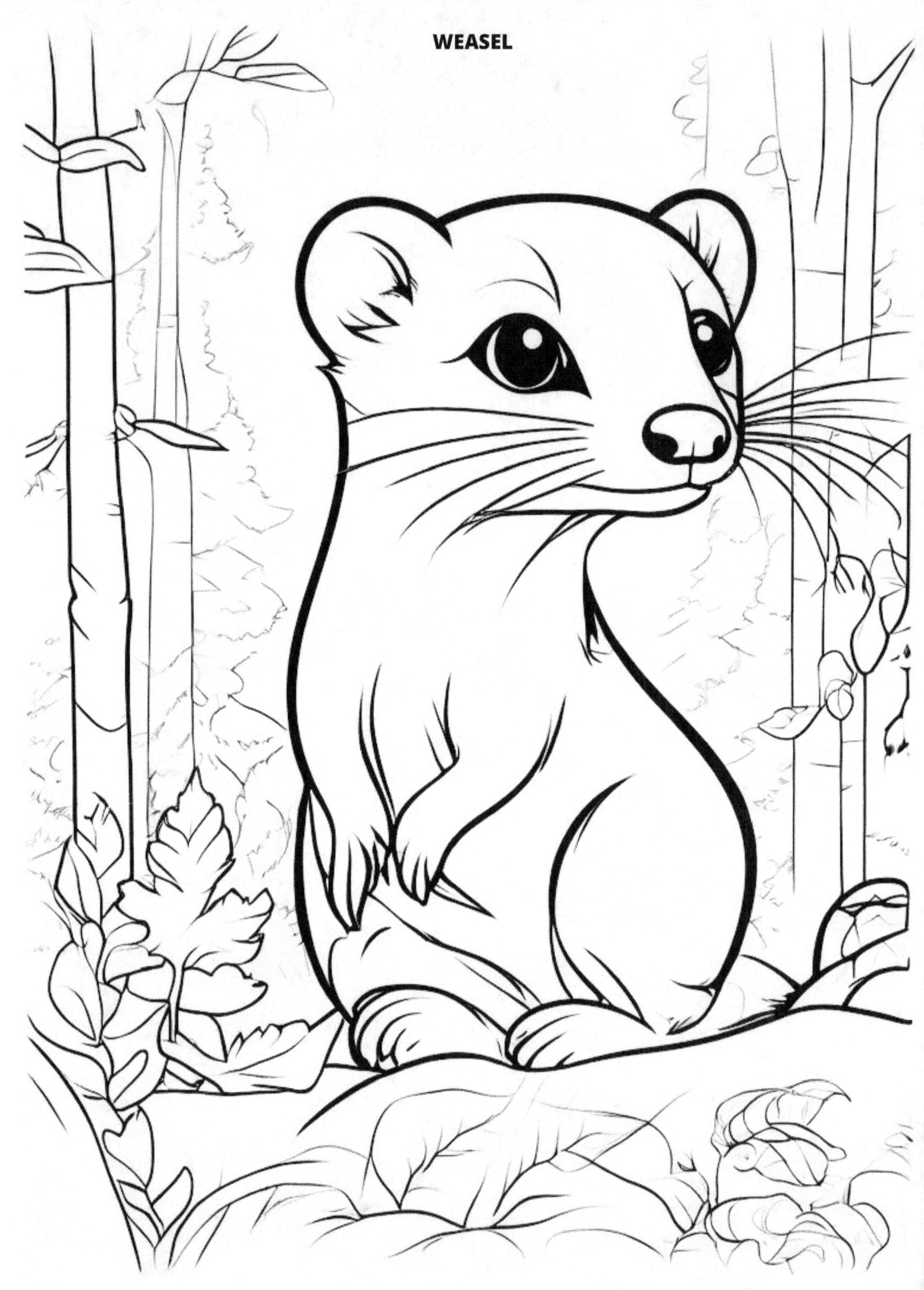

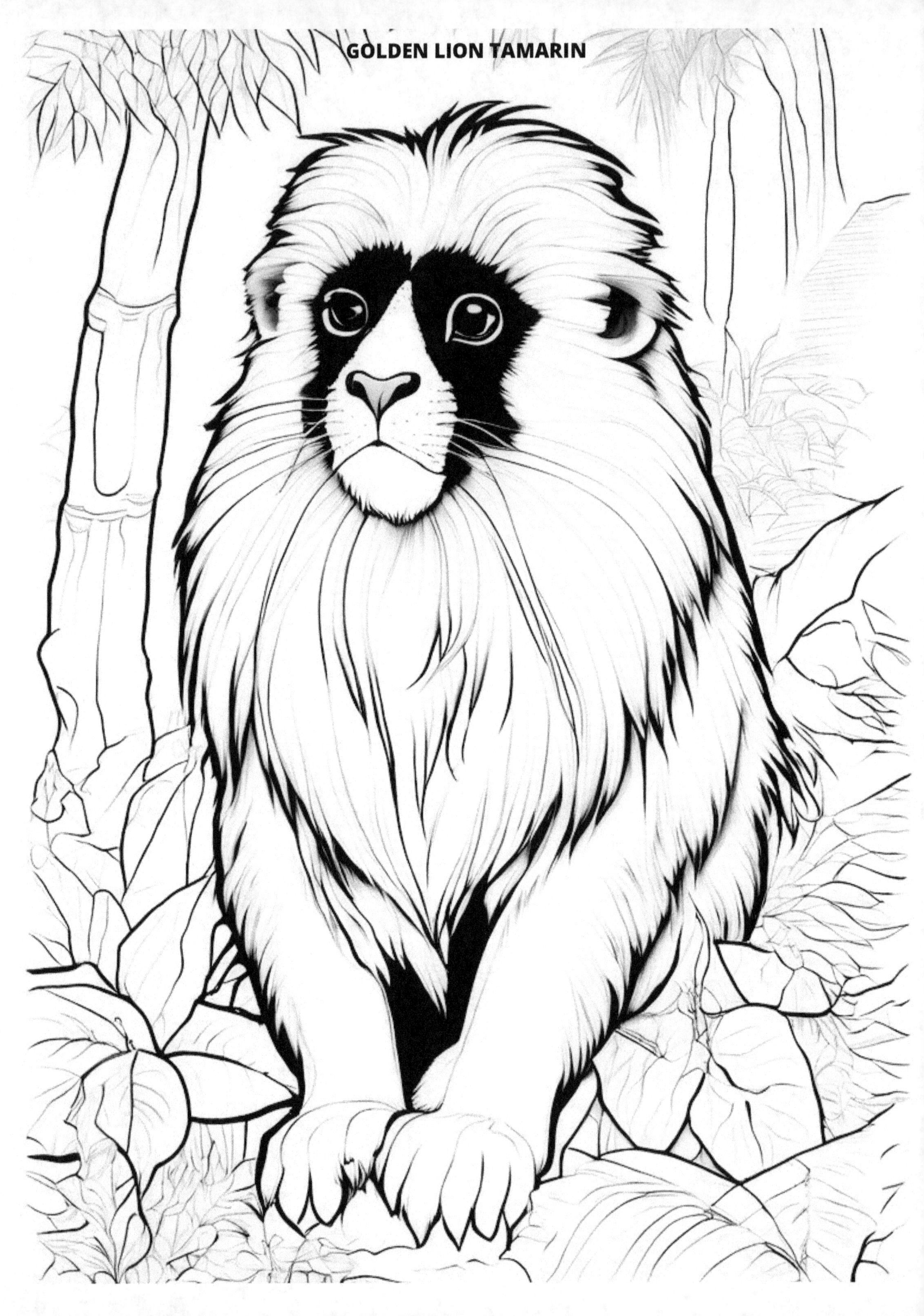
GOLDEN LION TAMARIN

WILD PIG

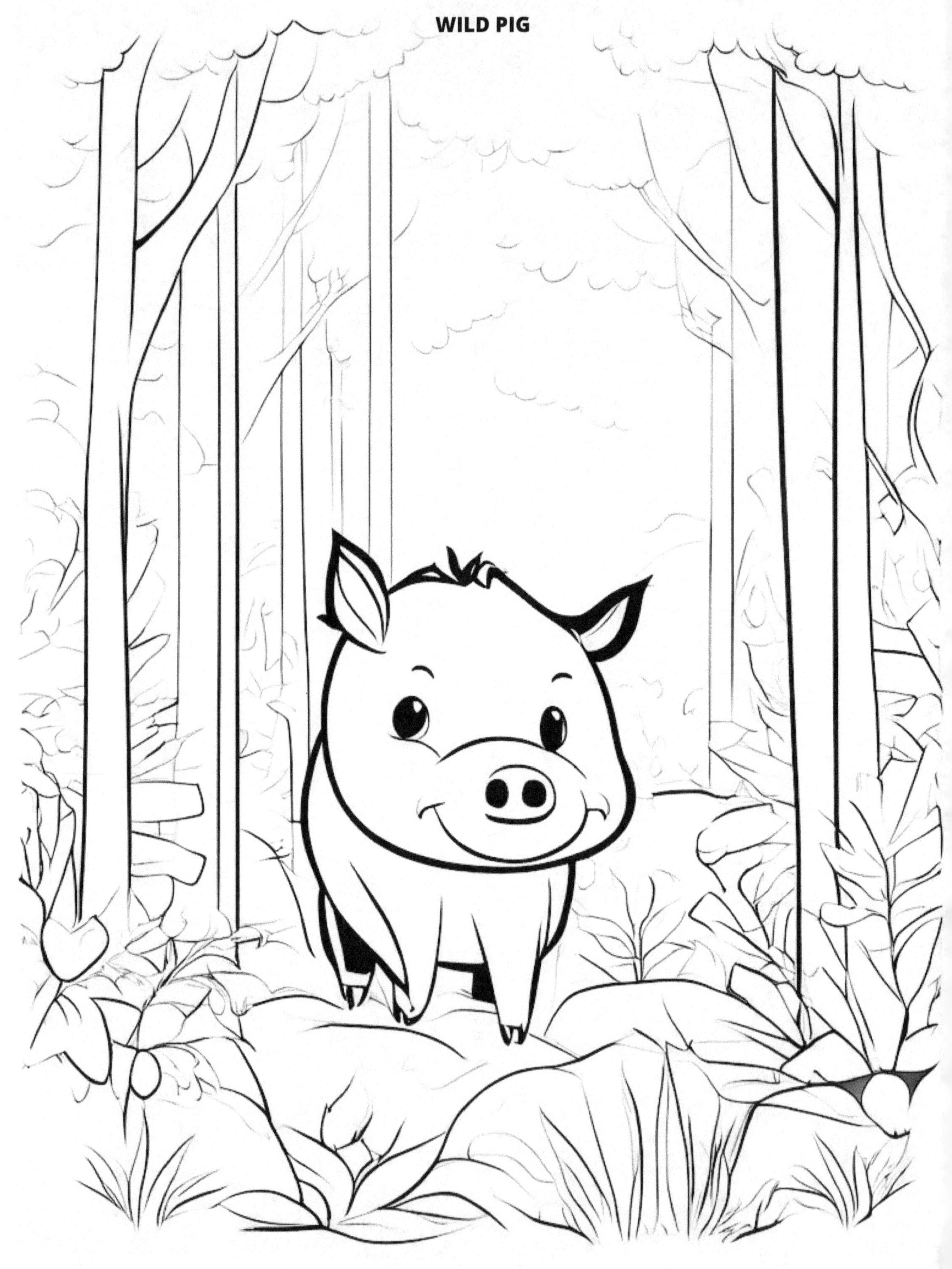

CUTE ANT

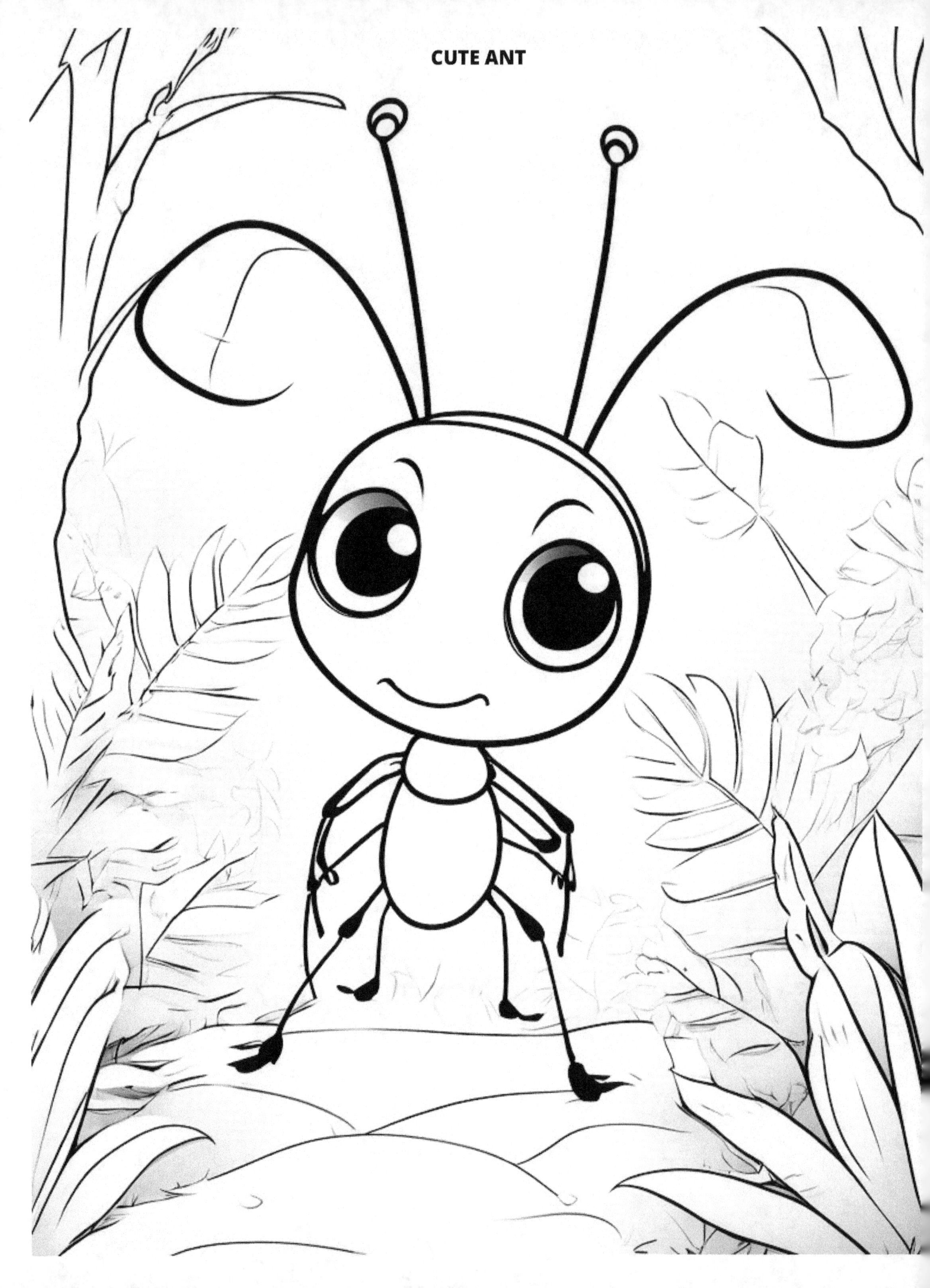

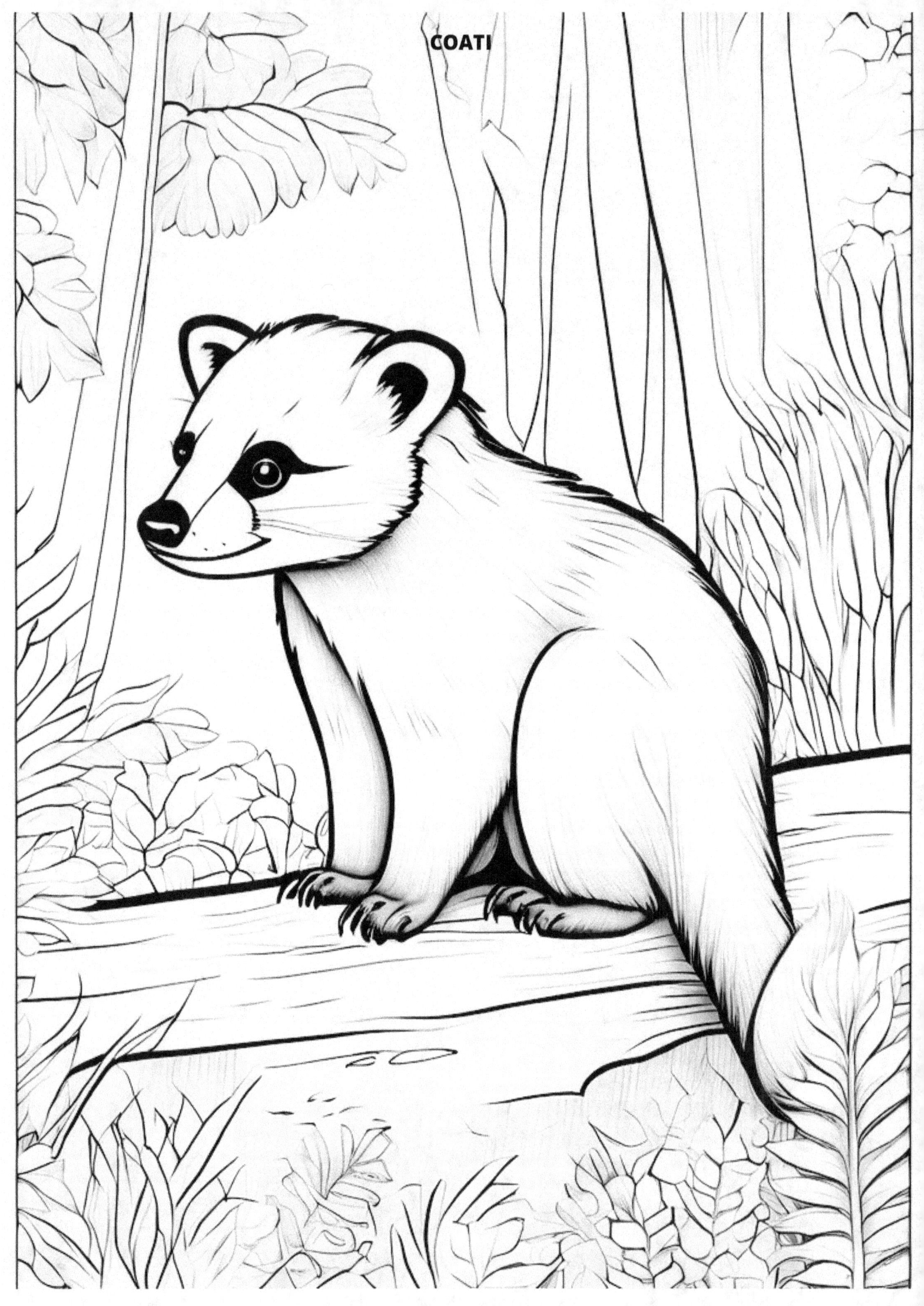
COATI